Praise for Healthy Land, Happy Families and Profitable Businesses

"I believe ranch sustainability has three legs: people, planet and profit. David Pratt covers each of these in this book as he challenges us to think, plan and rethink. If you are serious in wanting your ranch business to be successful/sustainable, then this is an important read."

Wayne Fahsholtz, Padlock Ranch President and CEO

"I have found that most ranchers would rather lose money conventionally than make money unconventionally. This book is not written for them. This book is written for people like you who have discovered that exceptional profits in ranching, or any field, come from thinking outside the box. This book will help keep your mind out there.

"There are a lot of good ideas in this book, many of which I plan to steal and use in my own business."

Allan Nation, Editor of The Stockman Grass Farmer

"For people who want to create healthy land, happy families and profitable businesses, this book is a wonderful primer packed with bite-size nuggets that go down easily and whet your appetite for more."

Fred Provenza, Professor Emeritus, Utah State University and Founder of BEHAVE

Praise for Healthy Land, Happy Families and Profitable Businesses

"A master storyteller, Dave Pratt explains, applies, and sticks the reader with the most profound insights you'll find in any farming business book. To have this much uncommon good sense packed into such a readable format is unprecedented. Because it condenses decades of experience into one volume, this book delivers more meaningful advice in a small space than I've ever seen. I'd want this one on my shelf even if I didn't have any others. What a delightful, wisdom-dense read."

Joel Salatin, Poly Face Farm

"Already in the introduction to Dave's book he makes it clear that his intent is to 'challenge the way people think and to help them see things differently.' If you will carefully read and seriously think about what you are reading, it will make a serious and important change in the way you look at and do things on your ranch. I know a good number of people who have taken The Ranching For Profit School and have been abundantly blessed for it. Some have been saved from the brink of bankruptcy; others have made a good business much better. They have done this while making ranching not only more profitable but more fun and rewarding. Everyone who is serious about improving the way they run a ranching business and wants it to be more enjoyable should read this book."

Burke Teichert, Teichert Management and Consulting

Healthy Land, Happy Families and Profitable Businesses

Essays to Improve Your Land, Your Life and Your Bottom Line

Healthy Land, Happy Families and Profitable Businesses

Essays to Improve Your Land, Your Life and Your Bottom Line

David W. Pratt

Ranch Management Consultants, Inc.

Library of Congress Control Number: 2013919144

ISBN 978-0-9910634-0-6

Published by Ranch Management Consultants, Inc.
Layout & Text design: Jill Blue Keith Co.
Cover Photo: Mery Donald
Printed in the U.S.A.

To Kathy,
for everything.

Table of Contents

Table of Contents

Table of Contents

Acknowledgements

No one ever does anything worthwhile alone. I am no exception to this rule. Stan Parsons opened my eyes to a new way of thinking about ranching. He was the most effective teacher I've had in my life and he opened the door to tremendous adventures, not the least of which was leaving the University to run Ranch Management Consultants.

Our small but effective staff at RMC liberates me to write and teach, free from worry about just about everything I don't want to worry about. My job description might be, "Do the things you enjoy." Theirs might be, "Do everything else."

My wife Kathy is not only the best life partner I can imagine but the best editor as well. Much more than making sure I use the right tense and fixing typos, she tells me when I haven't adequately developed a thought and reels me in when I start to ramble. She sometimes suggests cutting or re-writing text I thought was clear and clever. Her suggestions always result in a better article.

I am indebted to friends and colleagues Roger Ingram and John Marble and to my sister Robin Lynde for reviewing and editing this material. As a result, if you think this book is poorly written, blame them, but then imagine how much worse it could have been.

It is hard to know how to properly thank the thousands of *Ranching For Profit School* alumni and *Executive Link* members I've worked with and learned from. Seeing the principles we teach in the classroom applied to their ranches has been a fantastic experience. The people who come through our programs are self-selected to be those who are willing to invest in improving their ranches and themselves. I find their willingness to embrace change inspiring. When they come to *The Ranching For Profit School* and *Executive Link* they have a lot at stake and I am honored by the trust they put in us to assist them. They have taught me more than I have taught them.

Preface

Stan Parsons once wrote that ranching is "financially unattractive and economically unrewarding." He is right. Most ranches aren't profitable and only survive because we subsidize them. We subsidize them with off-farm income and by paying ourselves less than we'd have to pay if we hired someone else to do the work. We subsidize them with inherited wealth. (How many ranchers would be ranching today if they had to start their ranch from scratch?)

There is nothing wrong with subsidizing a ranch. But in spite of these subsidies, family-owned and operated ranches are disappearing at an alarming rate. According to the U.S. Census of Agriculture, there are 10% fewer cattle ranches in the United States today than there were just 20 years ago. Family ranches are becoming an endangered species. This trend underscores a fundamental problem: a ranch isn't sustainable unless it is profitable.

Ranch Management Consultants, is not out to save the world. We are out to save your ranch. Our mission reads: *Healthy Land, Happy Families and Profitable Businesses. Your* land. *Your* family. *Your* business. If you think that the word "save" is a bit strong, consider Kyle Marshall, who ranches with his wife, Kristen, in Burwell, Nebraska. Kyle and Kristen were about to join the more than 75,000 ranching operations that disappeared in the last two decades. When asked what difference our programs made to their operation, Kyle said, "We wouldn't be in business if we hadn't gone through that school. Things were that bad."

"That school" is *The Ranching For Profit School*, established by Stan Parsons in 1981. Through the school we have taught thousands of ranchers on five continents about economic planning, cell grazing and how to manage a family business. The school is based on a simple idea: knowing how to raise livestock is not the same as knowing how to run a *business* that raises livestock. We focus on the latter, not the former.

> A ranch isn't sustainable unless it is profitable.

Our alumni program, *Executive Link*, is based on two equally important concepts. The first is that when you are self-employed, you work for a lunatic. It's not a matter of intelligence or work ethic. The issue is accountability. If you are anything like the rest of us, you tend to work on the things you enjoy and the things you are good at. The problem is, those aren't always the things that need to be done. We can be so busy doing the $10-per-hour jobs that we never get to the $100- and $1,000-per-hour jobs.

The second concept is that it is almost always easier to solve our neighbor's problems than our own. We lack the objectivity to see our own situation clearly.

In *Executive Link* we organize *Ranching For Profit School* alumni into peer advisory boards. The boards follow a structured process to review each board member's business and provide experienced, objective input on the issues each member faces. Each member leaves the meeting with an action plan showing who will do what and when. At the start of the next meeting members are held accountable for the actions on their plan. One member summed up the difference this objectivity and accountability made to his ranch. He said, "Making million-dollar changes is what it boiled down to for us."

I've been writing *ProfitTips* (formerly called *ProfitPoints*) for nearly eight years. It began as a newsletter to keep our alumni thinking about *Ranching For Profit* principles and aware of upcoming events. Shortly after the first column we expanded the circulation to anyone interested in sustainable ranching. Twice every month a new edition of *ProfitTips* is sent to thousands of subscribers.

This book is a collection of re-edited *ProfitTips* articles sharing principles and practices that can improve the health of range and pasture land, improve the relationships in family businesses and increase the profitability of ranches. *Your* land. *Your* family. *Your* ranch.

I have nothing against saving the world; I just want to start with your place.

Healthy Land, Happy Families and Profitable Businesses

Essays to Improve Your Land, Your Life and Your Bottom Line

Introduction

What Have You Done to Me?

My mother and father divorced when I was young. My sister and I were raised by my mother on a small Northern California farm. Dee Whitmire, the Cooperative Extension Farm Advisor for our county, saw a family in need and got us involved in 4-H, me with sheep and my sister with dairy cattle. I was two years too young to join 4-H, but Mr. Whitmire bent a rule or two and found a way for me to participate. At the fair that summer, when most of the lambs were selling for 30¢ per pound, he arranged for someone to buy mine for $1 per pound. That was unheard of back then. A couple of weeks after the fair, he drove up to our house with three commercial ewes in the back of his truck. He told me that with the money I'd made, I could buy them if I wanted. That was my start in ranching. Mr. Whitmire helped guide a lost family on a positive path toward a brighter future.

Mr. Whitmire didn't help us because it would make him money, advance his career, enhance his image or make us indebted to him. He helped because he could. In fact, it was his job to help people. From those early years I thought, "What a wonderful job to have." So I set my sights on being an advisor with Cooperative Extension.

Fast forward 22 years. As a University of California Livestock and Range Advisor, my assignment was to help livestock producers solve the operational problems they faced by conducting research and providing training. I felt I was in over my head. Sure, I'd had courses in range management, reproductive physiology, ruminant nutrition, soils and agronomy. I'd even had courses in economics. I had practical experience working on our own place and as day help for commercial ranchers in our area. But in spite of my training and experience, I wasn't qualified to give my clients what they needed. In fact, I didn't even know what they needed.

1

That changed after I attended *The Ranching For Profit School*.

I'd heard about Dr. Stan Parsons and Allan Savory when I was a student working on my undergraduate degree in range management. My professors talked about Parsons and Savory as heretics who told ranchers to "rotate animals around in circles." Of course, that isn't what they were saying. They were offering a different way to manage land, animals, money and people. More importantly, they were proposing a radically different way to think about ranching.

Stan and Allan went their separate ways in the early 1980s. That's when Stan established Ranch Management Consultants and developed *The Ranching For Profit School* and *Executive Link*. After attending the school in 1988, I focused my research on the application of the *Ranching For Profit* principles to ranches in Northern California.

When I repeated the school the following year, I had two objectives. My first objective was to deepen my understanding of the *Ranching For Profit* principles. Repeating the school is like peeling the layers off an onion. Every time you attend you find new ideas and applications you didn't see before.

> "I cannot teach anybody anything; I can only make them think." *Socrates*

My second objective was to learn how to teach. When it came to teaching, Stan was a master and the classroom was his canvas. The school wasn't like any class I'd taken in college or any extension meeting I'd attended. Stan taught by asking questions and leading students to their own revelations. In addition to offering a lot of new ideas, he helped each of us look at our old ideas and experiences differently. It was the most effective learning experience I'd ever had.

You could have knocked me over with a feather when Stan asked me if I would be interested in teaching for him.

I taught my first *Ranching For Profit School* in 1992. The class was in New South Wales, Australia. I joked that Stan figured the further away from home I went, the more people would assume I knew.

After my first day teaching, Stan, who had been observing from the back of the classroom, offered me a beer and a debriefing. He began by asking me what I thought the purpose of the school was. I responded with something to the effect of "to give people the tools to build sustainable businesses." Stan slowly shook his head and said "no." He said the purpose was much more important than that. It was (and is) to challenge the way people think and to help them see things differently.

I wasn't convinced. Back then I didn't understand how just seeing things differently could be as important as learning the economic processes, applying the cell grazing principles or creating a strategic plan and holding people accountable to it. I do now. Nothing will change until you see things differently.

Our beliefs determine our actions. Our actions determine our results. Consider this pragmatic example. If I believe that big calves and high prices are the keys to making a profit, I will take actions that result in big calves and higher prices. On the other hand, if I believe that profit will be increased by building a business that mimics nature, and that profit has very little to do with weaning weights or prices, my actions will be very different. It all starts with changing the way we see ourselves, our ranches and the challenges we face.

Watching me teach that first school, Stan must have felt like he was watching his daughter go out on her first date with a Hell's Angel. But Stan continued to ask me to develop curriculum and teach schools for him. In subsequent years I taught *Ranching For Profit Schools* in the U.S., Canada, Mexico, Africa and Australia (in Australia it is called *Grazing For Profit*).

After one of the schools in Australia I spent a few days with Ian, a student from the class. Ian's wife drove from their home to pick us up at the school. As Ian drove us home he pointed to some tractors and farm equipment, saying, "Look at all of those fixed assets. Think about the depreciation costs he has from all that heavy metal every year." A few minutes later he pointed to a paddock on the other side of the road, saying, "There's grass in phase I and phase III side by side. That paddock must be understocked and overgrazed." We hadn't gone another kilometer before he nodded in the direction of someone spraying weeds and said, "He's treating symptoms, not getting to the cause of the problem." We passed two signs next to the driveway of another farm. One sign said "For Sale" and the other said "Farm Auction." Ian remarked, "There's someone who got stuck in a paradigm." Ian's wife looked at him like he was speaking a different language, which he was. When Ian saw her look, he turned back to me and exclaimed, "What have you done to me?" Ian was seeing things differently.

My hope is that the essays that follow will challenge your thinking about ranching. I hope they help you see yourself, your ranch and the challenges you face differently. That is the first step to healthier land, a happier family and a more profitable business.

1. Healthy Land

Hitting the Bull's-Eye
on the Right Target

Tom Lasater once said, "The livestock business is a very simple business; the complicated part is keeping it simple." We grow grass. Livestock eat grass. We sell the grass in the form of livestock (or the products that livestock produce). To do this profitably takes healthy pasture, an adapted animal and a production system that is in synch with nature.

The World at Your Feet

- Pay Dirt!

- Graze for the Grass Not for the Weeds

- Boots on the Ground

- Looking into the Land

- The Practical Side of Biodiversity

Pay Dirt!

The soil is alive! By weight, seventy to ninety percent of the organisms in a rangeland ecosystem live underground. Since we don't see them it is easy to forget them. Out of sight, out of mind. But healthy soil is more than just a bunch of dirt. Whether we see it or not, healthy, living soil is essential to a functioning ecosystem and sustainable profit. The key to creating and maintaining healthy soil is providing habitat and nourishment for the organisms that live there.

The soil is the plant's stomach. Just as microbes break down fiber in the cow's rumen, microorganisms in the soil break down fiber and other organic matter. As the microorganisms decompose organic matter they create humus. Humus is completely decomposed organic matter. It is essential in a healthy soil.

Humus stores nitrogen in the soil. In spite of all our scientific advances and technology, that's something we have not figured out how to do. Humus holds 30 times more nutrients than clay, absorbs six times its weight in water and increases oxygen availability in soil. The microbes that live in the humus attack soil pathogens. Humus is essential in a healthy soil.

Carbon makes things go

The primary food required by plants is the same as the primary food required by cows and sheep (and people). It is carbon. Carbon is energy. It makes things go.

Through the miracle of photosynthesis, plants take energy from sunshine, carbon from carbon dioxide (CO_2) in the air and water from the soil to produce starch, cellulose, sugars, proteins and other organic compounds. These substances are consumed by grazing animals and decomposed by organisms, releasing CO_2 into the soil. In nature, unless consumed by fire, nearly all carbon is recycled into the soil.

Maintenance of soil organic matter is important for many reasons, not the least of which is providing adequate carbon to feed the microorganisms. It is critical that sufficient crop and root residues be provided to replenish the organic matter. While nature returns nearly all organic matter to the soil, modern agriculture removes most of it. Farming and ranching will not be ecologically (or economically) sustainable unless we replenish and maintain soil organic matter.

Nitrogen makes things grow

If carbon makes things go, nitrogen makes them grow.

The atmosphere is 78% nitrogen, but plants cannot utilize nitrogen in gaseous form. In order to pass from the atmosphere to plants, and ultimately to animals and people, nitrogen must first be "fixed" by soil microorganisms. Even then, the complex protein molecules aren't available to plants until microbes break them down into ammonium and nitrate molecules.

Modern farming vs. pulsed (cell) grazing

The bottom line is that replenishing soil organic matter and maintaining a thriving microbe population are essential in any business that is ranching for profit. Unfortunately, most farming and ranching practices deplete organic matter and destroy humus. Australian scientist Christine Jones wrote, "Conventional farming (and ranching) techniques create biological deserts." Healthy grassland soils may have 4–5% organic matter. After only a few decades of modern grazing management and farming, they often have less than 1% organic matter. That is a problem, but it also offers a great opportunity.

According to Dr. Jones, "pulsed" grazing (short graze periods with adequate recovery period after grazing) adds organic matter to the soil and is the most effective grazing method for building and maintaining healthy soils.

Payday

I gave a presentation at a cattlemen's meeting in Reno, Nevada. It is appropriate that they met in Reno, because I showed them how some of their colleagues were hitting the economic and ecological jackpot.

As the world warms and carbon dioxide continues to increase in the atmosphere, interest grows throughout the world in trading carbon. Cell grazing offers tremendous potential to sequester large amounts of carbon in the soil. In fact, increasing the organic matter of the world's grassland soils by just 2% could return atmospheric carbon to pre-industrial levels.

A large portion of the carbohydrates produced through photosynthesis are stored in the root system of the plant. When the plant is grazed, the roots are "pruned," increasing the organic matter content of the soil. If plants are continuously grazed, the root growth is limited. But cell grazing, where plants are rested after being grazed, promotes root growth. This cycle of growth, followed by pruning, followed by growth, represents a "carbon pump" that removes carbon dioxide from the atmosphere and stores it in the soil. One of the benefits graziers get from this increase in organic matter is healthier, more fertile pastures with better rainfall infiltration and higher moisture holding capacity.

There is potentially a very nice payoff for skilled graziers. In fact, there are potentially two payoffs. First, by increasing the soil's moisture holding capacity, fertility and productivity, several *Ranching For Profit* alumni have dramatically increased their carrying capacity. One alumnus told me that it was like getting another ranch for free!

The second is a direct payment for sequestered carbon. While there are significant challenges to measuring stable soil carbon and developing markets for trading

> Cell grazing offers tremendous potential to sequester large amounts of carbon in the soil and earn significant income for skilled graziers.

carbon, some graziers are being paid to sequester carbon in the pastures they graze. Here's an excerpt from an email I received from a former *Executive Link* member in Saskatchewan:

> The thought of getting paid to graze for many is just a dream. With one of my landlords I have renegotiated the contract to split the carbon credit check. The thought process my landlord used is that, without my management using cell grazing, there would be no check. He gets compensated for allowing me to graze this way and I get compensated for the extra management. Plus, the stocking rate on this land continues to grow, so really this becomes a win-win situation. Everyone makes more profit.

Try to find odds like that in Reno.

Graze for the Grass Not for the Weeds

An article in a popular livestock publication described how people are using grazing for weed control. Sometimes they time the grazing to hit the weeds when they are most vulnerable. Sometimes they train the animals to prefer the weeds. I don't dispute that we can get livestock to graze the weeds and that doing so can be a valuable thing, but this strategy focuses on the symptom, the weed, not the core problem: the health of our pastures.

Somewhere along the line people started to believe that weeds make land unhealthy. But it is the other way around. Weeds appear *because* land is unhealthy. This is more than semantics. It is a major paradigm shift to accept that there is a difference between a weed-free pasture and a healthy pasture. The steps one takes to control the weeds (with a sprayer, a mower, or a critter) are fundamentally different than the steps one takes to produce a healthy pasture.

There are millions of viable weed seeds on nearly every acre of range and pasture land. The annual assault of weed seeds to our properties is huge and relentless. It may not solve anything to graze the weeds we see this year because more will grow next year. We need to change the conditions that allow the weeds to out-compete more desirable species.

Grazing weeds does not necessarily improve the health of desirable species, nor will it necessarily improve the water and mineral cycles or improve energy flow. If we manage grazing to favor these processes, weeds are unlikely to be an issue. Participants in *The Ranching For Profit School* see pictures of pastures choked with weeds where, in a very short time, desirable forages out-competed the weeds. The seed bank is still full of weed seeds. Weed seeds still fly in annually from the neighbors. But by grazing to improve basic ecosystem processes and grow

> Weeds don't make land unhealthy. They appear because land is unhealthy.

grass, rather than kill weeds, the desirables have been given a huge competitive advantage. We will save money, time and soil, and will reduce stress by focusing on the healthy pastures we want to create rather than on the weeds we want to kill.

Boots on the Ground

Sometimes ranchers who have implemented cell grazing and who want and expect to see improvements in the land say, "I'm seeing this new grass where I never saw it before!" The problem is, they may never have looked before. Our eyes and memories don't provide conclusive evidence of change. You've undoubtedly heard that "seeing is believing." But sometimes believing makes us see things that may not really be happening. Whether it is economic or ecologic, it is important to measure our performance and establish benchmarks. *Ranching For Profit School* alumnus Charlie Orchard tackled that challenge. Based on the principles we teach at the school, Charlie created *Land EKG*, which helps ranchers objectively measure the condition and trend of their land.

Looking *into* the land

You can't monitor the health of land from a windshield. You need to have boots on the ground.

> Our eyes and memories don't provide conclusive evidence of change.

Even then, we tend to look across the land rather than into it. Looking across gives us a distorted picture of what's really going on. We need to look into the land.

Study the photo on the next page. It was taken on a ranch in western Wyoming. The pasture on the left side of the fence hasn't had any livestock grazing in 12 years. The pasture on the right is grazed one week each year.

| Wildlife use but no livestock for 12 years | Grazed by cattle one week each year |

The ungrazed pasture looks like it has more cover, less bare soil and is generally healthier than the pasture on the right. But let's change our perspective and look down into the pastures, rather than across (*see photo below*).

 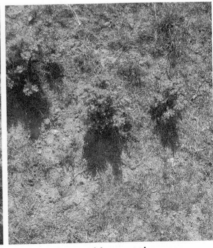

| Wildlife use but no livestock for 12 years | Grazed by cattle one week each year |

Now we see the real story. There is clearly more cover and less bare soil in the paddock with livestock grazing. The soil on the side with no grazing is exposed and it has formed a cap. A cap is a crust that forms when raindrops fall on bare soil. Capping reduces water penetration and increases runoff. There is more litter covering the soil in the pasture on the right and the soil is loose. When it rains, that litter intercepts raindrops so they don't hit bare soil. The litter slows the flow and increases infiltration. That grows more grass. Growing more grass increases the volume of roots in the soil. Those roots increase the organic matter in the soil, which further increases infiltration and moisture holding capacity.

There's more to the story

Fence-line contrasts often look impressive, but they can be misleading. In comparing these photos it would probably have been useful to know that cattle left the pasture with the one-week graze period the day before the pictures were taken! Imagine what the side-by-side comparison looked like a week earlier or what it will look like two weeks after the next rain.

The next time you drive down the road, before you draw too many conclusions about the health and productivity of your pastures, jump out and get your boots on the ground to see what's really going on. You might be surprised.

Looking into the Land

Looking into the land is pretty simple. As my son might say, "This isn't rocket surgery or brain science!" When we look into the land, there are four primary things we should consider:

1. The volume of energy flow through the community
2. The effectiveness of the water cycle
3. The effectiveness of the mineral cycle
4. Biodiversity

1. Energy flow

Energy flow simply refers to the volume of energy moving through the community. That starts with plants capturing energy through photosynthesis. To maximize that, we want 100% green cover for as long a period as is possible. We want broad leaf perennial grasses. Broad leaves are generally more efficient photosynthesizers than narrow leaves, and perennials stay green longer than annuals.

Once the energy is captured by plants, we want that energy to be available to other creatures, including our livestock and wildlife. But as plants mature, their protein content goes down and their lignin content goes up. Lignin makes the plant less digestible. This is a double whammy for grazing animals, because to break down lignin, rumen microbes need protein. Fortunately, extreme lignification can be prevented with good grazing management. However, for those stockpiling forage for winter grazing, some lignification is unavoidable. When cattle graze lignified grass, supplementing with small quantities of degradable protein can increase the energy animals get from that grass by 50%.

Up to 30% of the energy captured by grass plants is exuded through the roots as sugars, which provide energy for soil microbes. These microbes are an essential component of a healthy ecosystem. When they die and break down they release nutrients that the plants can use.

Over the last century, farmers and ranchers have come to resemble miners, extracting all the energy they can. That's not sustainable. Some of the energy must be left in the plant and some must be returned to the soil. Ultimately, humans and other animals can only survive on the photosynthetic energy in excess of that required to support the plant and the microbes. Get in line. The microbes come first.

2. **Water cycle**

Effective precipitation refers to the portion of rainfall that actually soaks in and is held by the soil. On many range sites less than half the rain that falls soaks in and is available for plant growth. On some sites it is much less than that. Most of the rain runs off, evaporates or percolates through the root zone. Of course, when it runs off it carries away nutrients and top soil.

Evaluating the effectiveness of the water cycle is pretty simple. We want to see cover and we don't want to see bare soil. That cover will intercept raindrop "bombs," preventing the soil from capping, and it will slow the flow of water over the surface, giving it more time to soak in.

3. **Mineral cycle**

If the mineral cycle is effective, minerals will be cycling rapidly and there will be several different types of plants. Different grasses, forbs, shrubs and trees root at different depths, extracting minerals from throughout the soil profile. The cycle continues as animals graze or browse those plants. The minerals the animals consume are used for growth, reproduction and other functions. The animal poops or pees the minerals it doesn't use as dung or urine. But the cycle isn't complete until the litter decomposes and becomes part of the soil. If the mineral cycle is effective, dung and litter on the soil surface will break down so rapidly that it will be hard to distinguish where the litter layer ends and the mineral soil begins.

Over-rested plants are a symptom of an ineffective mineral cycle. There may be plenty of minerals in their leaves, but the minerals aren't available to the animal because of the low digestibility. Stan Parsons described this bottleneck perfectly, saying, "The cows are standing belly deep in grass and starving to death." Another common bottleneck is the accumulation of dung and litter on the soil surface.

4. Biodiversity

Biodiversity includes the number of species, the genetic differences within those species and the number of habitats. While the importance of energy, water and minerals to support production is pretty obvious, the importance of biodiversity is less clear to most people. However, diversity is crucial to the health and resilience of the ecosystem.

"Species richness" is probably the most useful measure of biodiversity. Richness simply refers to the number of species occupying a range site. As part of his *Land EKG* program, Charlie Orchard has clients count up all the signs of different life in a specified area. Those signs could be obvious things, like a growing plant or dung, or they could be more subtle, like the call of a bird or the tracks of an ant. When it comes to health and diversity, the more the merrier.

A picture is worth a thousand words

One grazier I worked with several years ago had her eyes on a property where the previous tenant was booted out by the land owners. He'd nuked the place with cattle. What wasn't annual grasses and weeds was bare soil. When it rained the water didn't soak in. It ran off, carrying with it top soil and nutrients. Within a few years, what had been small creeks had become gullies. The owners, who were professional people living in the city and who bought the property as a retreat where they could relax and enjoy nature, were not happy. As far as they were concerned, the lease couldn't end soon enough. Needless to say they didn't renew it, and even vowed never to bring cattle on again.

Enter Shari. Shari met with the owners and told them that she had a tool that could reduce erosion and improve the water cycle. A tool that could reduce the weed infestation, increase vegetative cover on bare areas, restore native perennials and improve the wildlife habitat. When she told them that the tool was grazing, the same tool that had ruined the place, they were understandably skeptical. She explained the cell grazing principles, and then she showed them her photo album.

Shari had documented the changes she saw in the health of her own place by establishing some simple photo points. These before and after shots showed the owners that she could do more than just talk the talk. These pictures showed she had walked the walk. Some pictures may be worth a thousand words. Shari's pictures were worth a one-year lease at 40% of the rate the previous tenant had paid. Not knowing if she'd have the place beyond one year, Shari established a cell using temporary fencing. At the end of the year the owners were so impressed with the results that they extended the lease to five years and paid to replace the temporary fences with permanent fencing. Over the next three years Shari tripled the carrying capacity of the ranch.

Shari had been paying 40% of the going rate for rent, but having tripled the carrying capacity, she was paying the equivalent of 13% of the going rate per cow (40% ÷ 3 = 13%). That's a huge economic advantage—an advantage made possible by documenting the changes she'd achieved through cell grazing on her home place.

> Some pictures are worth a thousand words. Shari's photo point pictures were worth a lease at 40% of the going rate.

The Practical Side of Biodiversity

I once asked ranching consultant Gregg Simonds, "If there were only three things you could measure to evaluate the health of rangelands, what would they be?" He responded, "1. Cover, 2. Cover, and 3. Biodiversity." Gregg wasn't being facetious when he listed the top two criteria as cover. There are several types of cover (soil cover, basal cover, canopy cover, etc.). Cover is reasonably easy to measure, and I think most of us can appreciate its importance.

It is harder to understand or appreciate the importance of biodiversity. Biodiversity refers to the variety of plants, animals and microorganisms, the genes they contain and the ecosystems they form. Genetic diversity is critical to maintaining the viability of populations within species. Species diversity is vital for several reasons, not the least of which is the many interactive effects among organisms. For example, one gram of forest soil may have more than 4,000 different species of bacteria. The interaction of some of these bacteria with roots is essential for the vigorous growth of some commercial timber species. Some of these bacteria are dispersed by voles, mice, insects and other creatures we normally think of as pests. Without these microbes the trees don't grow as rapidly and are more susceptible to disease and pollution. It isn't a stretch to see the relationship between these rarely seen, easily forgotten organisms, the productivity of the forest and the jobs in the timber industry.

We will never know or understand all of the relationships between organisms in a community. We do know that when we lose diversity, communities are more susceptible to disease outbreaks, weed infestations and pest problems. Diversity also plays a role in the ability of an ecosystem to function during, and recover after, severe environmental events like droughts.

Cell grazing, which promotes root growth and creates habitat for desirable microbes in the soil, is just one of the many things we can do as ranchers to increase biodiversity on our properties. Avoiding excess fertilization and the use of toxic chemicals also tends to maintain or increase biodiversity. There are several things we can do to enhance habitat for wildlife that increase diversity. Wildlife waterers and ecological water troughs in which we promote the growth of reeds and other aquatic plants are terrific examples.

I've written about many *Ranching For Profit School* alumni who used their knowledge to drastically increase their carrying capacity without spending money on herbicides or fertilizers (which tend to decrease biodiversity) or seeding. What they feel for their land is not unique among ranchers. What they have that most of their neighbors don't is a deeper understanding of ecosystem processes and tools like cell grazing. The results we see consistently are more cover, more cover and more biodiversity.

The keys to ecosystem health are cover, cover and biodiversity.

24

Grazing the Grass Up

- Two for the Price of One

- The Nuts and Bolts of Cell Grazing

- Too Much Grass

- Not So Fast

- The Hay Is Stacked Against You

- Water Skiing Slowly

Two for the Price of One

Would you like a free ranch? I recently had the pleasure of visiting several *Ranching For Profit School* alumni ranches from Texas to Montana and points in between. Most are applying cell grazing and are producing impressive results. Cell grazing involves giving paddocks adequate rest, keeping graze periods short, using high stock density and adjusting the stocking rate annually and seasonally to match the carrying capacity. It is not a grazing system, but a set of principles that, applied with a little common sense, will improve the health and productivity of range and pasture in any grazing environment. John Schipf from Highwood, Montana, is one alumnus I visited this summer. He's been using cell grazing for about four years. He credits it for doubling the carrying capacity of his property. John said, "It's like getting a second ranch for free."

You'd think with these kinds of results, more people would be using cell grazing. Many ranchers say they rotationally graze. Most of them assume that because they move animals from one place to another that their pastures are getting healthier and they get some economic benefit. But most ranchers get little if any ecological or economic benefit from their rotations. In fact, most rotations don't even prevent overgrazing. A rotation with fewer than eight paddocks isn't rotational grazing. It is rotational overgrazing.

Rotational overgrazing

Overgrazing occurs when a plant is grazed before it has recovered from a previous grazing. There are two ways to overgraze: stay in a paddock too long or come back to the paddock too soon. It takes a minimum of eight to 10 paddocks per herd to give plants an adequate recovery period and also keep the graze period short enough so that the animals are gone by the time regrowth emerges on grazed plants. With fewer than eight paddocks per herd, you are rotational overgrazing.

Eight is not enough

Stopping the overgrazing is a start, but it isn't enough. During slow growth, when plants need more time to recover, the graze period can get pretty long if there are only eight to 10 paddocks. On the first few days of the graze period the animal gets its fill, but by the fourth or fifth day the quality and quantity of available forage drops, intake goes down and animal performance suffers.

It is pretty well accepted that grazing animals will eat roughly three percent of their body weight in forage on a dry matter basis. Following that rule you'd expect a 700 pound steer to eat about 21 pounds of forage in a day. But like many rules, there are exceptions.

The graph below shows typical daily forage intake for stocker cattle on irrigated pasture during a five day graze period. Steers may eat five to six percent of their body weight on the first day in the paddock (35-42 pounds of forage for a 700 pound steer). That will usually drop to only one or two percent by the fifth day of the graze period (7-14 pounds of forage for that steer). Intake over the five days averages three percent, but the extreme boom-or-bust diet that we get with long graze periods is likely to result in mediocre animal performance at best.

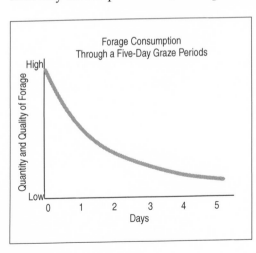

Forage Consumption Through a Five-Day Graze Periods

The second graph shows typical daily forage intake when animals are moved every two days. As with the longer graze period, animals may eat five to six percent of their body weight on the first day of the graze period. That typically drops to about three percent on the second day.

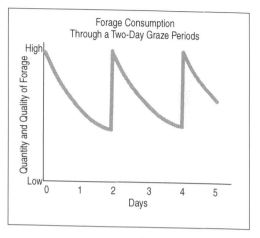

The average intake over the two days is four percent. Which animals would you expect to perform best, the ones that eat more or the ones that eat less? You got it: short graze periods tend to improve animal performance.

The critical factor in giving pastures adequate time to recover *and* keeping the graze periods short enough to support good animal performance is the number of paddocks per herd. We usually need at least 14 to 16 paddocks per herd to support good performance.

For someone not familiar with cell grazing, that may seem like a lot of paddocks, but you'll find many *Ranching For Profit School* alumni using 25 or more paddocks per herd. While you can stop overgrazing with eight to 10 paddocks per herd, and support good animal performance with 14 to 16 per herd, it generally takes 25 or more paddocks per herd to promote rapid range improvement and to dramatically increase the carrying capacity, especially in drier environments.

If 25 paddocks seems like a lot, just wait. I had the pleasure of spending an afternoon with Emry Birdwell and Deborah Clark on their ranch near Henrietta, Texas. They run stocker cattle in big herds. Last year they started with three herds of 1,500 head, using 50 paddocks per herd … that's right, five-zero.

As the severity of the drought increased, they realized that to give the grass more rest and keep graze periods short, they'd be better off combining the herds. They wound up with 4,500 cattle in one herd, moving through 150 paddocks. When I was there they were moving the herd twice a day. By lengthening the rest, keeping graze periods short and increasing stock density, Emry said they were able to get an extra month of grazing from the ranch before they destocked. It also decreased their work load. It takes less time to move one herd of 4,500 animals than it does three herds of 1,500.

The benefits of running one large herd have been so big that, drought or no drought, Emry and Deborah are continuing to run all the steers in one mob through their 150 paddocks. When I visited they had 3,500 in the herd, with plans to expand in the coming weeks to 5,000.

To some people, having 25 paddocks per herd, let alone 150 paddocks per herd, seems impossibly complicated. Our experience is exactly the opposite. It simplifies management by offering graziers more control and more options as to where and when to graze. Having more paddocks doesn't constrain management. It makes management possible. Others assume that moving animals more frequently will increase their work load. But since most people combine herds, the amount of labor required often decreases. It takes longer to check three herds of 200 animals than one heard of 600.

Even if it were more labor, it might be worth the effort. Many of our alumni using cell grazing see big increases in carrying capacity. Most of them are using at least 25 paddocks per herd. Some, like Emry, use a lot more.

8–10 paddocks per herd stops overgrazing.
14–16 paddocks per herd supports good animal performance.
>25 paddocks per herd are required for rapid range improvement.

The Nuts and Bolts of Cell Grazing

The Nuts and Bolts of Cell Grazing

In response to an article I wrote about developing a grazing cell on my sister's irrigated pasture in Northern California, I received emails from ranchers in Florida, British Columbia and just about every state and province in between. The gist of the emails was, *Sure, cell grazing would work there* (any environment they aren't in), *but it won't work here* (whatever environment they are in). Actually, only a few were negative. Most genuinely wanted to know if cell grazing practices that worked in a place where the carrying capacity was a cow to an acre could be applied to rangelands where the capacity was 50 acres (or more) to a cow.

The five basic cell grazing principles that apply on my sister's irrigated pasture also apply to rangeland, but the way you apply them will change. The principles are:

1. Provide adequate recovery for plants after grazing.
2. Use short graze periods consistent with the required recovery period.
3. Use the highest stock density practical.
4. Use the largest herd consistent with good husbandry.
5. Match the stocking rate to the carrying capacity annually and seasonally.

1. Provide adequate recovery for a paddock after grazing

Overgrazing is grazing a plant before it has recovered from a previous grazing. The recovery period that plants need depends on the growth rate. The growth rate depends on the season (moisture, temperature, day length, etc.) and the severity of the previous grazing.

The challenge in dry environments is simply to grow enough grass. I don't feel sorry for anyone in the West who has too much grass, even if the quality of that grass isn't very good. We can find ways to use even low quality grass. The single biggest mistake people make in grazing management in dryer environments is providing too little rest.

In wetter and more humid environments, the focus changes. It is relatively easy to grow grass. The challenge is maintaining its quality. Because growth rates tend to be faster in these environments, the recovery periods are generally shorter. Shorter recovery periods keep forage palatable and nutritious.

During the spring flush of growth in dry environments, a recovery period of 30 to 60 days is probably in the ballpark. During the rest of the year, recovery periods of three to 10 months may be needed. With irrigation, my sister gets growth for more than six months out of the year. Her recovery periods vary between 30 and 50 days during the growing season. Her rest periods are 60 to 100 days during the slow-growth period. She may graze each paddock five or six times in a year. On dry rangeland you are more likely to graze a paddock twice a year. Some rangelands may only be grazed once a year.

2. **Use short graze periods consistent with the required recovery periods**

Here there is really no difference between irrigated ground and rangelands. We want to keep the graze period short. Short graze periods ensure that animals don't take a second bite just when the plant is starting to recover from a previous grazing. Keeping animals moving to fresh feed keeps them on a higher plane of nutrition, improving their performance.

3. **Use the highest stock density practical**

Stock density is the number of animals per acre at a particular time. Increasing density will increase the uniformity of grazing.

When I talk about stock density I talk in terms of the number of animals per acre, but I'm actually thinking of the number of mouths per acre. More mouths increase the uniformity of grazing.

4. **Use the largest herd consistent with good husbandry**

One animal walking the same path every day for a year will create a trail where the soil is compacted, the soil surface is hard, water will concentrate and run off and nothing will grow. Move 365 animals in a herd all at once and the impact will be very different. While the stocking rates in both scenarios is the same (365 cow days), when the herd is moved all at once the soil surface will probably be loose and covered with trampled vegetation. Below the surface the soil will not be compacted. Water will penetrate more easily and not be as likely to run off. Months after the herd passed, the vegetation could be even thicker than it was before. The impact of a large group of excited animals is called "herd effect."

Everything else being equal, it is easier to stimulate beneficial hoof action (herd effect) with big groups of animals than with smaller groups. The easiest way to get big herds is to combine lots of little herds. This has the added benefit of increasing stock density and making more paddocks available per herd. With more paddocks per herd, you'll be able to get the rest you need with shorter graze periods. It is also less work to check one herd of 400 animals than four herds of 100. Of course, if you build one large herd you'll need to make sure you have the water storage and delivery capacity to handle larger mobs.

Herd effect is controversial in academic circles, but just ask cell grazing practitioners and they'll tell you what an inexpensive and effective tool it can be. They have used it to jumpstart successional processes, to break capped soil and to promote a shift from weeds to more desirable species.

One hundred years ago naturalist John Muir wrote, "In the planting of her wild gardens, Nature takes the *feet* and teeth of her flocks into account and makes use of them to trim and *cultivate* ..." Perhaps one of these days academia will catch up with Mr. Muir.

5. **Match the stocking rate to the carrying capacity annually and seasonally**

In other words, match the demand (stocking rate) to the supply (carrying capacity). It is that simple ... and it is that challenging. It is simple because it is just common sense. It is challenging because carrying capacity changes both annually and seasonally.

On rangeland the annual carrying capacity will fluctuate more than on my sister's irrigated pasture. The bigger the annual fluctuation, the more important it is to make sure your enterprise mix is compatible with the drought risk. In drought-prone country we need enterprises that can be destocked quickly. Enterprises that are harder to destock should be stocked only to a conservative level.

The carrying capacity also changes seasonally. Fortunately, animal needs also change seasonally. Cows require more in the six weeks before calving and in the first couple of months of lactation than they do in late lactation and after weaning. Synching the production cycle to the forage cycle, or using seasonal enterprises to use the flush of growth early in the growing season are effective strategies for matching the stocking rate to the carrying capacity.

> The single biggest mistake people make in grazing management is providing too little rest.

If there were a sixth principle it would be to be flexible in the way you apply the other five. Cell grazing is not a "grazing system." It is a management method. Systems imply rigidity. Turn cell grazing into a system (e.g., move every two days) and you have the recipe for a wreck.

Rest periods need to change as the growth rate of plants change. Short graze periods, which improve the plane of nutrition for the animal, are most critical when animal requirements are high. High stock density is always nice, but is most important during the dormant season, especially if you are rationing stockpiled forage and trying to eliminate the need for hay.

Sometimes you may sacrifice the grass for the animal. For example, you may decide to shorten graze periods to flush animals prior to breeding, even though it may mean shortening the recovery period on some pastures for a while.

Sometimes you may sacrifice the animal for the pasture. For example, during the dormant season, even though your animals want to move to fresh feed, you may hold them a day or two longer in each paddock to lengthen the recovery period.

Sometimes you may sacrifice both the animals and the pasture for personal needs. If you have a child in the emergency room, keeping animals in a paddock for an extra day or two is a small price to pay. Need a vacation? Open a bunch of gates and set stock for a month. You can get back on track when you come back. Cell grazing doesn't give you the mandate to manage; it gives you the opportunity to manage.

• • •

After reading this article one rancher asked why I used *mouths per acre* as the unit for measuring density rather than *pounds of animal per acre*.

You will hear some people talk about stock density in terms of the weight of animals per acre. In my opinion they are making things more complicated than necessary and possibly less meaningful. Consider a herd of 400 dry, pregnant cows weighing 1,300 pounds and grazing a 50-acre paddock. I'd say the density is eight cows per acre (eight mouths per acre):

$$\frac{400 \text{ cows}}{50 \text{ acres}} = 8 \text{ head} / \text{acre}$$

Someone figuring the weight per acre would say the density is 10,400 pounds per acre:

$$\frac{400 \text{ cows x 1,300 pounds per cow}}{50 \text{ acres}} = 10,400 \text{ pounds per acre}$$

I don't mind the math. Here's my problem. What if instead of four hundred 1,300-pound dry, pregnant cows, I had four hundred 500-pound steers gaining about 1½ pounds a day? The energy those steers need to gain 1½ pounds a day is roughly equal to the energy those cows need to maintain themselves. By my way of reckoning, eight head per acre is the same stock density whether it is steers or cows, and we can expect roughly the same uniformity of use. Cows or steers, it's the same number of mouths.

If we are using animal weight per acre, we would say that the stock density with the steers is 4,000 pounds per acre.

$$\frac{400 \text{ steers x 500 pounds per steer}}{50 \text{ acres}} = 4,000 \text{ pounds per acre}$$

That's less than 40% of the stock density you'd have with the cows even though the number of mouths per acre are the same. I'll bet you those steers don't reduce the uniformity of use by 60%.

Certainly we can't equate sheep mouths with cattle mouths, but somewhere along the line we need to apply a little common sense.

On irrigated pasture it is reasonably easy to get high densities. I've used densities of up to 700 head per acre for very short periods of time. I know others who have used well over 1,000 head per acre. The result is very uniform use of paddocks. The problem on rangelands is, because the carrying capacity is so low and paddocks are much bigger, the stock density is much lower. Even so, high stocking rate or low stocking rate, higher densities will improve the uniformity of utilization.

• • •

Another reader asked if stock density could be too high. He wrote, "Is there a point that sees more grass trampled due to very high density and less consumed by the animal, leading to lower animal performance and carrying capacity?"

That's a good question, but you can't get stock density too high. You can keep them in a spot too long, or put them under too much stress, but the density won't be too high. Stress is a question of handling, infrastructure design, weather and other environmental factors.

A lot of people confuse stock density with "herd effect." Herd effect is the concentrated impact of the herd, and that's what creates the trampling. High density increases the uniformity of use in a paddock but doesn't necessarily create herd effect. There is often a little herd effect happening near the gate as the animals come into the paddock. But once in the paddock and grazing, even with high stock density, there shouldn't be much herd effect.

Trampling further out in the paddock shouldn't be an issue if animals are moved with minimal stress. In the ideal scenario, animals shouldn't be charging into the next paddock. They ought to be walking and they ought to stop once they are through the gate to graze. Ideally, they should only move on when the critter behind them says, "Mooove over. I want some too."

I'm no livestock handling expert, but I saw Bud Williams work and have worked with enough of his students to think that you may want to consider gathering the herd and bringing them up to the gate with the gate closed. Then, when you open the gate, lead them into the paddock. Once they start coming in, move back and forth perpendicular to the flow of the herd. This might be on foot, horseback or a four-wheeler, depending on the size of the paddock and the size of the herd. This back and forth movement should slow or stop the herd's movement so they stop walking and start grazing.

Oregon grazier John Marble wrote that he believes the feed "lost" to trampling is primarily a function of time, not stock density. John says that when the graze periods are short, "the only plants that aren't eaten are at dung and urine spots. Long graze periods yield more 'lost' grass."

Too Much Grass

Each spring I get questions from people about handling the spring flush of growth. *I've got a problem: I've got too much grass. How do I keep up with it?*

There is no such thing as too much grass. I don't intend to minimize the challenges of dealing with the spring flush of growth, but the problem isn't too much grass. The issue is the imbalance between the seasonal carrying capacity and the stocking rate and the decline in forage quality when the forage gets rank.

These are challenges every producer faces in every grazing environment. There are many environments where fast growth lasts less than a month, making it impractical if not impossible to match forage demand to the supply. Knowing that most graziers share this challenge probably doesn't help much, unless misery really does love company. But this isn't a problem that should make anyone miserable. Our attitude ought to be, *Oh boy! I've got too much grass.*

Accept it. You can't keep up with fast growth, and that's okay because having too much grass is better than not having enough. The rank grass left after the flush may be low in protein and high in lignin, reducing its digestibility, but that's okay too. Using a supplement high in degradable protein (e.g., urea), you can give the rumen microbes a boost so that they can make more of the energy in that lignified feed available to the cow. Having a lot of low quality grass is better than having no grass at all.

Yes, effectively managing the spring flush can be challenging. Here are some alternative strategies for managing the spring flush:

1. Graze the grass up! You have to make deposits in your feed bank before you can make withdrawals from it. Make deposits by keeping graze periods short (consistent with the recovery period) and grazing lightly. Leaving a lot of

photosynthetic material behind will keep plants growing rapidly. Light grazing during the growing season keeps plants vegetative and can stimulate new tillers to grow from axillary buds at the base of the plant. Short graze periods also keep the animals moving to fresh grass frequently, which supports good animal performance.

2. Consider adding a short-term (100 days or less) stocker enterprise or some other grazing enterprise to use the spring flush of growth.

3. Open the gates and set stock during this period. A lot of people think that fast growth is the time to get more intensive with your grazing management. The opposite is true. A Kiwi friend, and terrific grazier, uses eight paddocks per herd during rapid growth, but breaks each paddock into five strips during the dormant season. That makes a total of 40 paddocks per herd during the dormant season.

4. Take a couple of paddocks out of the rotation in May and June and cut hay (preferably with someone else's equipment or some kind of share cropping arrangement so that you don't have to own the equipment or provide the labor). Either way, sell your share of the hay. Just because you grow it doesn't mean you need to use it. At today's hay prices your cattle probably can't afford to buy it.

> "You'll never go broke having too much grass."
> Bud Williams

5. Synchronize your production schedule with the forage cycle to match changes in your animals' nutritional needs to the seasonal changes in carrying capacity. In seasonal stocker enterprises this may mean selling your heavier calves as grass growth slows down.

When in doubt ask, "How does this problem play out in nature?" Helping nature do what comes naturally is usually a key to addressing issues like this profitably.

Not So Fast

I helped my sister build a grazing cell on her farm on the western edge of the Central Valley in Northern California. The short story is that the grass is greener and there is more of it than there used to be. In spite of an extremely dry spring, she reduced her winter feeding by six weeks while carrying more animal units than ever.

Several months after building the cell, I asked her what she liked best and least about the cell. She said that the lower costs from reducing her reliance on hay and the improved pasture health were the biggest benefits. When I pressed her for disappointments or difficulties, she was stumped. She wasn't able to come up with any. She did say that the thing she found hardest was having the discipline to stick to her grazing plan, especially when growth starts to slow down. Using 24 paddocks with three-day graze periods gives each paddock 69 days of rest. But after two days in a paddock, the best forage has been grazed and the flock wants to move. Seeing lush forage in the next paddock, Robin says she's been tempted to move them.

It's hard not to succumb to SBES (Sad Brown Eye Syndrome) when the sheep promise her that each one of them will have unassisted twins next year if she will move them today, just one day early. But knowing that sheep lie (cows lie too), Robin said she's stuck to her guns and resisted moving them early. She said she realized that moving just one day sooner would mean losing more than three weeks of rest in each paddock by the time she returned. She knew that if she deprived the pastures of those three weeks of rest the grass wouldn't be so lush next time around.

Moving too fast will lead us into a vicious cycle: we are out of feed so we move. The problem is, we are out of feed *because* we moved. You don't grow more grass by moving animals faster. You grow more grass by providing more rest, and that means either moving animals more slowly or subdividing paddocks.

A half-hour after we spoke, Robin called me back to tell me that she had thought of a negative to cell grazing. She'd gone out to the paddock to move the flock and came back with a hand full of fiberglass splinters. She moves a couple of fiberglass posts that hold up the flex net gate each time she moves her flock. We used a cheap grade of fiberglass and as those posts weather they get rough. If you don't wear gloves they can give you painful splinters. I didn't see a big problem with the splinters since I wasn't the one moving the fence. Robin said that the problem wasn't the splinters. The problem was forgetting her gloves.

> Moving too fast leads us into a vicious cycle: we are out of feed so we move. The problem is, we are out of feed because we moved.

The Hay Is Stacked Against You

If you want a profitable ranch and you feed hay for more than a couple of weeks out of the year, the odds are stacked against you.

There's a big difference between *supplement* and *substitute* feeding. *Supplementation* makes up for deficiencies in forage *quality* and improves gross margin. *Substitution* makes up for deficiencies in *quantity*. Feeding hay is substitute feeding. The problem with substitute feeding isn't just the cost of the feed. It's also the cost of the labor and equipment it takes to do the *feeding*. Substitute feeding increases overheads and drains profits.

In most environments, the amount of hay required can be drastically reduced, if not eliminated, by synching the production schedule of your animals with the forage cycle.

> Supplementation makes up for deficiencies in forage quality. Substitution makes up for deficiencies in quantity.

There are limits to this. Anyone with snow up to their eyeballs for four months out of the year who thinks they can eliminate hay by shifting the calving season better think again. The only way to get the hay out of an operation like that is to create seasonal enterprises. That's how nature would do it.

If the snow doesn't get too deep (over 2 feet) and the crust isn't too severe for too long, winter grazing ought to be feasible. Rationing forage during the dormant season to minimize or eliminate the need for hay is one of the most profitable aspects of cell grazing.

Leaving leaves

Some folks have a hard time imagining grazing in the winter because they haven't left anything to graze. To get the hay out of an operation we have to build a feed reserve during the growing season. That reserve must carry us through the dormant season until growth begins again.

Bud Williams once told me that ranchers treat their grass like it was their enemy. "As soon as it starts to grow, most people feel like they need to graze it down." If you don't want to have to feed hay, you need to learn to graze it up! Grazing it up means grazing to keep forage growing rapidly throughout the growing season. Since most of the energy for regrowth comes from whatever leaves are left on a plant after grazing, severe grazing during the growing season will severely limit the amount of grass you are able to stockpile. Short graze periods that just top the plant and leave lots of leaves will keep plants growing rapidly throughout the growing season. When Nebraska rancher Marlene Moore moves her cattle out of a pasture during the growing season, there is still a good foot of green, growing residue in those pastures. She leaves lots of leaves.

The time to get intensive

Consultant Jim Gerrish has it right when he talks about *management*-intensive grazing rather intensive *grazing* management. He puts the emphasis where it belongs, on the management. Most people think the time to get intensive is when things are growing fast. But it is pretty easy to grow grass during the growing season. The challenging time to manage grass, and the time of year that is most important to get intensive with your management, is the dormant season.

During the dormant season our grazing strategy changes. We focus on rationing the grass we've accumulated during the growing season to make it last until the growing season starts again. Now we graze the grass down. Because growth is slow to non-existent, we need very long rest periods. To get those rest periods, graze periods either have to be lengthened or the number of paddocks increased. Increasing the number of paddocks per herd is generally the preferred option since it has the added benefit of increasing stock density. Higher stock density will improve the uniformity of grazing. Increasing paddock numbers per herd doesn't necessarily mean building more paddocks. The number of paddocks per herd can be increased by combining herds. A lot of places have one or more seasonal herds (e.g., stockers, custom grazing) that leave the ranch toward the end of the growing season. If that's the case, those paddocks can now be added to those used by the cow herd.

Reading the dung

Stockpiled forage is often low in protein and high in lignin, making it less digestible. The result can be inefficient utilization and poor animal performance. Supplementing lignified forage with a little degradable protein can make a big difference in forage utilization and animal performance. Marlene Moore calls her stockpiled grass her "hay pile" and the wheat grass that grows up through it in the spring her "protein tub." During late fall and the dead of winter, nature's protein tub may not be available and, if that's the case, a little supplementation with degradable protein may be called for.

An easy and reasonably accurate test to see if animals are digesting forage effectively is to look at their dung. If the fiber length in the dung is short (3/8 inch or less), the rumen microbes are effectively breaking down the fiber. If fiber length is longer, microbial activity can be stimulated, forage utilization improved and livestock performance increased by supplementing small amounts of degradable protein.

Break glass in case of emergency

As much as I encourage people to find ways to eliminate the need to feed hay, I still think people who intend to graze year-round in country with severe winters ought to have hay. My hope is that they won't need to feed it. But in case there's an emergency, a blizzard with unusually deep snow, or a crust of ice so thick over the stockpiled feed that it can't be broken even with herd effect, you'd be well advised to have hay as insurance.

That hay may still come from your own place. It may make sense to cut some hay during the spring flush of growth. However, it probably doesn't make sense to cut it yourself. Few ranchers have enough hay land to justify owning the equipment. It is generally much more profitable to hire someone to put it up or to buy it from off the farm. Remember, this is the emergency hay pile. The quality doesn't have to be high.

Water Skiing Slowly

Several years ago when I was still with the University of California, I met with a rancher who had a massive weed problem in his irrigated pasture. He wanted to know what he should spray to kill the weeds. He had four mobs of sheep. Each mob was rotated through four paddocks. He'd heard that short graze periods keep animals on a high plane of nutrition and can improve animal performance, so after grazing each paddock for two days he moved to the next paddock. That provided six days of rest before each pasture was grazed again. What he was calling a grazing rotation was actually an overgrazing rotation. As soon as the plants in a pasture started to recover from grazing, the animals were back to graze them again. No wonder he had weeds.

There were several problems with what he was doing, not the least of which was the rigidity of his program. As growth rates changed through the season, he should have been varying the recovery periods between grazings. The other big problem was that the short grazing period he was using made the rest period way too short.

If he combined all of the animals into one big flock he could have increased the rest to 30 days and kept his two-day graze periods, at least when pasture growth was fast. That would have also quadrupled the stock density, which would have resulted in more uniform use in the paddocks. While I felt that this was a reasonable solution, I didn't think he'd go for it. So I suggested he combine the flocks into two groups, each using eight paddocks, and lengthen the rest period. Eight to 10 paddocks with adequate rest would stop the overgrazing.

I happened to be talking to Stan Parsons, the man who founded *The Ranching For Profit School*, on the phone that evening and told him about the rancher I'd met with that day. Rather than water down the recommendation to something acceptable, he very rightly said I owed it to the rancher to let him know what I really thought. Stan said my advice was akin to telling the rancher to "water ski slowly." Can you imagine, never having water skied, to tell the boat driver to go slow? You'd just get wet and never get up on your skis. While eight paddocks per flock could have stopped the overgrazing, graze periods would have been too long for optimum animal performance and the density would not have been high enough for good pasture utilization.

Realizing that Stan was right, I visited the rancher the following day and told him that combining all four flocks was the best alternative. Stan's advice has stuck with me. It is easier and more honest to say what you think. I don't know if the rancher combined the flocks or ever changed his grazing program, but after I suggested he combine all four flocks into one he asked me, "Now what should I spray?" You can lead a rancher to water, but you can't make him ski.

> Taking half-measures usually gives us all of the costs of both alternatives but few of the benefits of either.

Doing Things Right vs. Doing the Right Things

- Give a Calf a Bath

- Less Can Be More

- Slaughtering Another Sacred Cow: Higher Prices Don't Always Mean Higher Profit

- Low-Cost Strategy Is the Most Profitable

- Square Pegs and Round Holes

Healthy Land

Give a Calf a Bath

A calendar published by a USDA agency offered month-by-month suggestions for making livestock operations more efficient. One recommendation for January caused me to do a double take. It suggested that when new-born calves freeze to the ground, producers should "place them in a warm bath." Give the calf a bath? Of course! Why didn't I think of that? I would have probably dressed it in a cozy jacket or bought portable heaters to put out in the paddock. A bath makes much more sense.

A calf bath is a great idea because it opens up the door to lots of new and interesting products for ranchers to buy. Perhaps a supplement company could market calf bath salts. Someone will undoubtedly start selling Brahman bath bubbles. To increase species diversity maybe we could add a rubber ducky.

Of course, nature's calves have no such advantages. In fact, I wonder what happens to bison calves, or fawns or elk calves when they freeze to the ground. Oh, that's right, they don't freeze to the ground because THEY AREN'T BORN IN JANUARY!!!

An alumnus repeating *The Ranching For Profit School* in Calgary said that after attending the school and changing the calving season, he didn't bother to check the cows at calving. In fact, he said he put the cows in the pastures farthest from the headquarters at calving so he wouldn't even be tempted to check them. He said if a cow couldn't deliver a live calf on her own, he didn't want her or her calf to be part of his herd. He figured the cost of saving her and her calf exceeded the value of saving them.

Another attendee, who calved in February, said that he considered it cruel not to check the cows at calving. He'd seen too many calves frozen to the ground. Isn't that backwards? Animals have given birth without man's assistance (or interference) for ages. But then, they don't give birth in January and February. Isn't it more cruel to put an animal in a situation where it might freeze to the ground? I guess not, if we have the bath water drawn.

> If a cow can't calve on her own she shouldn't be part of the herd. The cost of saving her and her calf often exceeds the value of saving them.

Less Can Be More

Effectiveness trumps efficiency. It isn't important to do something efficiently if you shouldn't be doing that thing. Agriculture is replete with examples.

Reproductive efficiency

I spent an evening with Bill, a former *Executive Link* member, who told me about his shift from February to June calving. He said he has reduced his substitute feeding to only the most severe weather, and some years doesn't feed any hay at all. He provides only a mineral and a little degradable protein seasonally so his cows can get the energy they need from his stockpiled grass. He said that at less than $60 per cow, his direct costs are a fraction of what they were when he calved in February. Last year he weaned an 85% calf crop and made a healthy profit doing it.

Bill's neighbor, who is not a *Ranching For Profit School* alumnus but has been on our mailing list for several years, invited us over for a beer and started asking questions. When Bill said he weaned an 85% calf crop, the neighbor scoffed and bragged that his weaning rate is usually 95%. His cows calve in March. Not surprisingly, he feeds a lot of supplement and substitute feed. After a little napkin math I showed him that his feed costs were nearly $500 per cow, $440 higher than Bill's. That's $440 per cow to wean 10 more calves per 100 cows. That's $4,400 for each of those extra 10 calves!

Big calves

"But I wean much bigger calves than Bill," he argued. At 600 pounds, his calves were about 150 pounds heavier at weaning than Bill's. For every 100 cows, he weaned 18,750 more pounds than Bill.

(85 calves x 150 extra lbs.) + (10 calves x 600 lbs.) = 18,750 lbs.)

With a little more napkin math I showed him that his cost of gain for those additional pounds was $2.35 per pound. To rub salt in the wound I added, "Of course Bill's lighter calves are probably worth about 20¢ per pound more than your heavier calves." If a 600-pound calf brings $1.50 per pound for a total of $900, and it would have brought $1.70 per pound when it was 450 pounds for a total of $765, then the value of the last 150 pounds it gains is only 90¢ per pound.

$$\$900 - \$765 = \$135$$
$$\$135 \div 150 \text{ lbs.} = 90¢ \text{ per lb.}$$

As a group, North American ranchers are the most productive in the world. We wean bigger calves and more calves per cow than anyone else, anywhere else. We are hitting the bull's eye, but we are aiming at the wrong target. We have been focused for so long on increasing productivity that we don't realize less can be more ... less productivity can mean more profit.

> We are hitting the bull's eye, but we are aiming at the wrong target.

The productivity paradigm is deeply ingrained. I recently asked a workshop audience, "If I showed you how to lower costs by $250 per cow, but you'd be weaning smaller calves and your income would drop by $50 per cow, would you be interested?" One participant (speaking for several, I fear) emphatically said, "No!" When I asked why he'd forgo the $200 per cow improvement to the bottom line, he said, "I wouldn't be as productive." Apparently his bottom line is productivity, not profitability.

The most productive business is rarely the most profitable.

Slaughtering Another Sacred Cow: Higher Prices Don't Always Mean Higher Profit

What are the three things that ranchers discuss every time they get together? The weather, prices, and the #%&$# government. What are the three things you can't do anything about, at least in the short term? You got it. The weather, prices and the #%&$# government. Of course these things are important, but wouldn't our time be better spent working on things we can control rather than complaining about things we can't?

Since 1970, input costs have risen five times faster than cattle prices. That trend has led some to use low prices, rather than their ineffective management, as an excuse for poor profitability. I've heard more than a few ranchers lament, "We'd be profitable if only the prices were fair." You'll get no argument from me that it

> Provided you receive near-average prices for your calves, there are many things more important than calf prices influencing your profitability.

would be easier to make a profit in the cow/calf business if calf prices were higher, but the price we receive for our calves does not dictate our profit. I have proof.

Benchmark businesses (businesses that earn a double-digit ROA) with cow/calf enterprises <u>do not</u> receive more for their calves than their less profitable neighbors. According to our data, they often receive slightly less for their calves.

If it isn't the income per calf, what makes these benchmark businesses so much more profitable than their neighbors? There are several factors:

1. Almost all of them calve later in the season than their neighbors. They understand that the wintering cost of cows has more influence on profitability than calf prices. By stockpiling forage and matching their cows' lowest

nutritional requirement to their worst feed conditions they dramatically reduce their costs.

2. Benchmark businesses may receive a slightly lower than average price for the class of animal they are selling, but they generally aren't selling the same class. Their weaned calves may be 150 to 200 pounds lighter than their neighbor's. Their smaller calves don't produce quite as much income per head as their neighbor's larger calves, but on a pound-for-pound basis they are worth much more. They know that as the calf grows, each additional pound it gains is worth less than the previous pound.

3. Younger, lighter calves don't use as much pasture as older, heavier calves. That leaves more forage to carry more cows. Faced with a choice of increasing weaning weights by 100 pounds or running 10% more cows, they choose running more cows.

4. They may not sell those light calves at weaning but retain them in a stocker program to take advantage of the flush of growth next spring. Their stocker program also gives them a relatively simple way to destock in drought without culling into the genetic core of their cow herd.

5. They know that higher prices almost always come with higher costs. A recent market report showed that organic calves were worth 50% more than conventional calves, but organic hay cost 100% more than conventional hay. Before jumping at the higher prices offered by branded beef programs, benchmark producers evaluate the cost that participating will add to their operation. They know that the higher price they can receive does not always compensate for the higher costs they may incur.

6. They manage their cull cow program. They know that cow depreciation is the biggest cost of keeping a cow and that the cost of replacements, cow longevity and the cull cow market have at least as much influence on profitability as calf prices. Cow depreciation tends to be highest when calf prices are up. This doesn't mean we ought to pray for low prices. It means there are factors other than the price of calves that may be of equal or greater impact on your profitability. Unfortunately, it isn't nearly as sexy to talk about cull prices as it is calf prices.

Weaning weights and calf prices distract us from more important issues like keeping overhead costs low, improving the gross margin per unit and increasing turnover.

I'm not suggesting we should become complacent about marketing or wish for low calf prices. Higher prices will make most ranch businesses more profitable, provided we don't spend too much to secure those prices. A rising tide floats all boats. But only the low overhead producers with strong margins based on low cow costs, not high calf prices, will continue to earn a profit when the tide goes out and prices fall. Provided you receive near-average prices for your calves, there are many things more important than calf prices influencing your profitability. Prices don't determine profit.

Low-Cost Strategy Is the Most Profitable, but You Can't Starve a Profit into a Business

The most productive ranches may not be the most profitable ranches. In fact, according to our benchmarking, they are often among the least profitable. Ranches with extremely high cow productivity generally rely on a lot of inputs. Their input and inputting costs are often greater than the value of production attributable to the inputs. An *Executive Link* member summed up why the low-cost strategy is generally the most profitable strategy in ranching using the following example:

Imagine a cow/calf operation that produces $100,000 of income and incurs $80,000 in costs. It makes a profit of $20,000. Cutting costs by $20,000 (25% of $80,000) will double profit from $20,000 to $40,000. You can also double the profit of the business without changing the cost structure, but you'd have to increase the scale of the business by 100%. In other words, you'd need to grow the business from $100,000 of income and $80,000 in expenses to $200,000 in income and $160,000 in expenses.

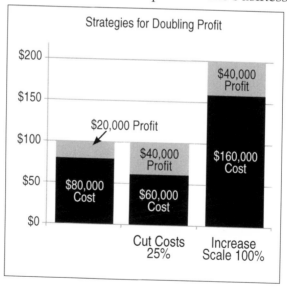

59

Here are a few questions you may want to consider as you choose the strategy that holds most promise for you:

1. Which strategy requires less labor?
2. Which strategy requires less capital investment?
3. Which strategy involves less risk?
4. Which strategy will be more profitable if cattle prices go down?

Of course, if you pursue the low-cost strategy and *then* increase the scale of the business, profit is quadrupled. But first things first, and the first thing is to build a low-cost business.

While the low-cost strategy usually wins, the lowest cost strategy may backfire. Just as you can't spend your way to profit, we mustn't be penny wise and pound foolish. Small things can make a big difference. For example, we eliminated hay feeding on a California ranch by stockpiling pasture, rationing our winter grazing and providing a fall/ winter supplement with degradable protein for just under $20 per cow. The degradable protein stimulated rumen microbes so that they would more efficiently break down lignified forage. By spending $20 per cow on supplement, we improved the gross margin by nearly $200 per cow.

> Spending your way to profit is like trying to borrow your way out of debt.

The essence of the livestock business is converting solar energy into harvestable animal products. Our goal should not be to maximize productivity or minimize costs. It should be to optimize the economic efficiency of this conversion. In the proper amount, at the appropriate time, a few inputs can go a long way to improve this conversion. Stan Parsons, the founder of Ranch Management Consultants, was right when he said, "You can't starve a profit into a business." Nor should we try.

Square Pegs and Round Holes

There's more and more talk these days about low input, and even no input, ranching. Some people make the assumption that reducing inputs always increases profit, and that if reducing them is good, eliminating them is even better. Unfortunately, as explained in the last article, it isn't quite that simple, it isn't always true and it may be distracting us from a more important issue.

The structure of your business, including the enterprise mix and production schedule, dictates the inputs needed to produce the maximum sustainable profit. Consider a typical commercial cow/calf operation calving in March and April. It's likely that we'd be able to find cuts that could increase profit, but we can only go so far unless we are willing to tackle some big questions. Should we have cows? If we should, then should they be here all year or seasonally? Should they be our cows? What calving season is best suited to this environment? (These are all questions you are challenged to answer at *The Ranching For Profit School*.)

The answer to these core questions for one Nebraska alumnus was, "Yes. We should have cows and they should calve in May." Having shifted the calving season to be in synch with the forage

> You can push a square peg into a round hole, but it is expensive. Increasing profit starts with finding a peg that matches the hole.

cycle, they drastically reduced the need for substitute feeding. Not having to feed hay all winter meant not having to irrigate, cut and bale it all summer. That dramatically reduced their overhead costs, not to mention their stress.

The next challenge was to find the most profitable replacement strategy. They asked if they should raise their own replacement heifers, like most other ranchers, or buy them. The breakthrough came when they realized that replacements didn't have to be heifers and that since they were calving later, they could buy the neighbor's late-calving cows much cheaper than they could either raise or buy replacement heifers. An added bonus was that the extra effort most people exert calving first-calf heifers became a non-issue. By purchasing bred cows instead of raising their own replacements, and changing a few other management procedures, they were able to dramatically improve the gross margin per cow and reduce labor.

High inputs often result from having an enterprise mix and production schedule that doesn't fit the environment. You can push a square peg into a round hole, but it is expensive.

Increasing profit starts with finding a peg that matches the hole. When we focus on getting the right enterprise mix, production strategy and organizational structure, the input costs usually take care of themselves.

Ranching with Nature

- It's Calving Time?

- In Synch

- The Cull Cow Business

- To Worm or Not to Worm

- The Case Against Genetics

- The Search for the Perfect Cow

It's Calving Time?

The February 11 headline of a major online beef magazine reads, "Calving Season Takes Off." Calving season takes off on February 11?

The article says *"… we all face the same issues: snow, mud, cold ears, assisting heifers, tagging and weighing newborns, updating record books, cleaning out calving barns, maintaining cow health and keeping calves from getting sick."* That's because the calving season takes off in February!

The reality is that we don't all face those issues. In fact, ranchers who have realized that working with nature is more profitable than fighting nature may not face any of them. Let's look at each of the issues "we all face."

Snow, mud, and frozen ears

Nature times the calving and fawning of wild grazing animals to avoid snow, mud, and frozen ears.

Assisting heifers

Research from the University of Nebraska shows that later calving also decreases calving difficulties.

Tagging, weighing, and updating record books

Most of the records most ranchers keep are a waste of time. We spend 90% of our time collecting data and less than 10% figuring out what the data means. We ought to reverse those proportions. Even then, the records we keep rarely show progress relative to a plan. In the absence of a plan, record keeping is just busy work.

A lot of people keep "to do" lists. In Jim Collins' best-selling book *Good to Great*, he recommends that business people develop "stop doing" lists. Most of the records most ranchers keep should be added to their "stop doing" lists.

Cleaning out calving barns

They wouldn't need to clean the barn if they didn't have a barn. They wouldn't need the barn if calving were in synch with nature. Perhaps as long as they have a barn, it can be put to more profitable use boarding horses, storing antique cars for other people or giving the volunteer fire department some practice.

Maintaining cow health and keeping calves from getting sick

Matching the two most stressful times in an animal's life (being born and giving birth) to the most stressful environmental conditions is asking for problems. In fact, we create or exacerbate some disease problems by calving out of synch with nature (e.g., Foothill Abortion and Grass Tetany).

> "I think Nature is smart as hell. I help as much as I can, but I try to let her do most of the work."   *Tom Lasater*

One size does not fit all

I spoke to a rancher from Colorado recently who had prepared a defense of his March calving season for me. He told me he typically has more than 2 feet of crusted standing snow for more than four months every year. He was sure I was going to argue that he ought to be calving in May or June. He was mistaken. Shifting the calving season would not dramatically change his need to substitute feed in the winter. It is unlikely that nature would have had grazing animals in that country in the winter at all. A better question than, "When should I calve?" would have been, "Should I even have cows and should they be here year-round?"

Tom Lasater, founder of the Beef Master Breed, once said, "I think Nature is smart as hell. I help as much as I can, but I try to let her do most of the work." Conventional management, summed up in the magazine article, strives to do the opposite. This strategy has resulted in high costs and low profit. Lasater's philosophy is a key to profitable ranching.

In Synch

Have you ever seen a fawn born in January or February or an elk calf born in March or April? Ever seen either born in October, November or December? I bet you haven't. Photoperiod has a big influence on the reproductive cycle of all grazing animals, including cattle. How big an influence depends on the latitude. According to grazing nutritionist Dick Diven, at 45°N (e.g., Baker City, Oregon; Dillon, Montana; Aberdeen, South Dakota) a cow in body condition score 5, calving in February, will take an average of 82 days to start cycling. It will take an identical cow calving in June only 40 days. The further north we go, and the more extreme the difference in summer and winter day length, the more profound the influence.

The first estrous cycle after a cow's post-partum interval is her least fertile. We'd like to make sure that her second cycle, or preferably her third cycle, falls within the 365-day window to increase the odds of getting a calf from her every year. Add a cow's 21-day estrous cycle to the 82 days before her first cycle and you'll see that it takes the cow calving in February more than 100 days after calving to start her second estrous cycle. It takes roughly 60 days for the cow calving in June.

That February-calving cow has a problem. The gestation period of a cow averages 280 days. If a cow is going to produce a calf every year, she has only 85 days to rebreed (365 − 280 = 85). Clearly the winter calving math doesn't add up.

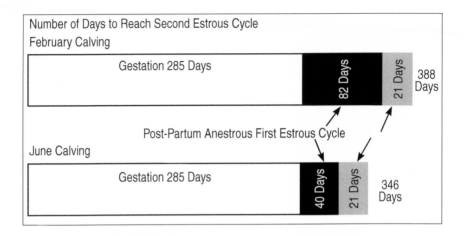

Number of Days to Reach Second Estrous Cycle

It takes an average of 388 days for the February-calving cow to reach her second estrus cycle and 409 days to reach her third. It takes the June-calving cow an average of 346 days to begin her second cycle and 367 to begin her third.

In spite of the numbers, many ranchers are reluctant to change their current calving season. One *Ranching For Profit School* alumnus who thought about changing the calving season wound up changing only after he slipped on the ice when he was heading out to start up his tractor to bring hay to the herd. He broke his leg, and his wife wound up feeding the cows for the rest of the season. She declared they were never going to calve in the winter (March) again. The next year, they calved in May and June.

Of course, changing the calving season isn't going to matter if we have snow up to our eyeballs for five months out of the year. Before we determine the ideal calving season for our cows, we need to ask if we ought to have cows in the first place. And if so, should they be our cows?

If we decide that cows are a good fit, photoperiod is just one of the considerations that should influence your production schedule. In California's annual range, calving in May or June would be a disaster. March and April are likely the ideal months. In tall fescue country, calving when the deer give birth could be a problem because of fescue toxicity.

One Missouri alumnus asked me to "remind people that when we make big changes, our cows don't like it." He had moved his calving season from March to May and when he preg-checked the herd he found that he had a lot of open cows. He remarked that he calved in March because May and June were good months for cows to breed. But then he added that he knows he can't profitably calve in March due to the expense of hay making and feeding. He went on to say, "We need to remind folks that we'll have to change cattle types, not just turnout dates … big changes, even in the right direction, may still carry some bitter short-term consequences."

Making structural change, like changing enterprises or shifting production schedules, will have ripple effects through your whole business and can't usually be done as isolated actions. They affect our susceptibility to market risk and drought. They require that we revisit our supplementation, health and marketing programs, and challenge the most basic assumptions we make about our ranches.

For example, most people who are thinking about calving later start with the assumption that they should make the transition with their own cattle. (After all, our cows are always better than everyone else's.) But your herd was selected to perform in your current production scheme, not the new system. You may find that selling your productive winter calving herd and replacing it with other people's late calvers is a more profitable strategy. These late calvers already fit the new schedule. Does this tactic introduce problems? Of course it

> If we have snow up to our eyeballs for five months out of the year, selecting the right calving season isn't our biggest question. Our biggest question is, "Should we have cows?"

does, but it also knocks most, if not all, of the depreciation out of the herd. (In most herds, depreciation is the single biggest cost of keeping a cow.)

May and June calving has been a breakthrough for a lot of people, but it isn't right for everyone or for every environment. John Muir said, "When one tugs at a single thing in nature, he finds it attached to the rest of the world." That is certainly the case when you make a structural change like changing the calving season.

The Cull Cow Business

The typical beef cow has only three calves in her lifetime. Most people have a hard time accepting that. They remember the cows that had calves every year for the last 10 years. But the average is three. To prove it, just do the math.

A typical replacement rate on a well-run ranch is 20% (the national average is higher). It's not hard to imagine a 20% replacement rate. That would be 1–2% that died, 4–6% that palpated pregnant that didn't wean a calf, 6–10% that were open and another 5–10% that were culled because they were too big, too old, too mean, too (fill in the blank). Add that up and you have to keep 16 to 28 replacements to maintain a herd of 100 cows. Twenty percent is less than the industry average.

Using a 20% replacement rate, let's see what happens to 100 bred replacements over four years:

	Opening Inventory	20% of Opening Inventory	Number of Original Cows Left
1st Year	100	-20	80
2nd Year	80	-16	64
3rd Year	64	-13	51
4th Year	51	-10	40

After three years, only 51 of the original 100 cows are still in the cow herd. Forty-nine of them had three or fewer calves in their life! At the end of four years, only 40 of the original bred replacements are left. That's why cow depreciation is the biggest cost of keeping a cow for most ranchers and why the cow/calf business is really the cull cow business.

$$\text{Cow Depreciation} = \frac{\text{Replacement Cost} - \text{Salvage Value}}{\text{Cow Longevity}}$$

Depreciation on most ranches varies from $150 to $300 per cow per year, depending on cattle prices. When calf prices and replacement costs are highest, cow depreciation also tends to peak. When cattle prices are low, depreciation tends to be low too.

The cow/calf business is really the cull cow business.

If you have cows and want to make a profit, you'll have to find a way to reduce cow depreciation. Several *Ranching For Profit School* alumni have eliminated depreciation from their cow herds. Here are three things they've done:

1. Reduce replacement costs.
    Bud Williams used to say that we don't make our profit when we sell animals; we make it when we buy them. That is as true with cows as it is with stockers. If you are like most ranchers, you may be able to buy replacements for a lot less than you can raise them, especially if you calve later than your neighbors. Their open and late-calving cows may be a good fit for your late spring- or summer-calving herd. (No one ever said that replacements had to be heifers.) Of course, in buying your replacements, you have a lot less control of your herd's genetics, but that may be a cheap price to pay for the benefits, which include:
    - Substantial savings on replacement costs
    - Drastically reduced cow depreciation
    - Not having to calve out first-calf heifers
    - Not having to re-breed H2's

2. Get more for culls.

 Your culls are probably more than twice as heavy as your calves. A 10-cent-per-pound swing in the cull market has more impact on the income per animal than a 20-cent-per-pound change in calf prices. Whether it's more effective marketing or breeding your open cows to fit someone else's calving season, look for strategies to increase the value of your cull animals.

3. Increase the average number of calves that cows produce in their lifetime.

 You'll only go so far with this strategy. Remember, a cow on a ranch with exceptional reproductive performance is unlikely to have more than four calves in her lifetime.

Depreciation is the biggest cost in most cow herds, but it doesn't have to be the biggest cost in yours. The key to reducing it is accepting that the cull cow business is not just part of a profitable cow/calf business but potentially the most profitable part.

To Worm or Not to Worm

I was helping my sister worm her sheep last weekend. (More accurately, I was keeping her company while she did the work.) I don't remember what she was using. I don't keep track of that sort of thing. She's got a small flock of about 50 Jacob ewes with more than 80 lambs. Jacobs have two or four horns and, as a former sheep shearer, they make me glad I'm a *former* shearer. Busy as always, Robin had a lot to do and was not thrilled with the prospect of having to worm the ewes. I asked Robin why she was worming them. "Because they have worms," she said. Then she added, "This is what the vet recommended."

We started talking about what might happen if the ewes and lambs weren't wormed. I'm sure productivity would drop, especially on some of the ewes, but other ewes would probably be less affected. This raises some interesting questions. Would the benefit of selecting a relatively parasite resistant animal be worth the cost? What would it cost (e.g., lower reproductive rates, lower weaning weights, higher culling rates) to select parasite resistant animals? Would 40 ewes be a big enough population to do this kind of selection? Geneticists tell me that it is pretty hard to have a genetics program with fewer than 400 animals. I don't know what kind of success a producer like my sister, working on a much smaller scale, would have.

Tom Lasater, founder of the Beef Master breed of cattle, once wrote, "More emphasis has been placed on medication than on breeding trouble-free cattle, with the result that, to some extent, United States producers have bred the vigor out of their cattle." We protect our animals from cold, heat, drought, too much rain, parasites, rough terrain, predators, poor quality feed and many other problems. The result is that we have created animals that need protection.

Lasater didn't recommend eliminating the vaccination program. He recommended vaccinating only against diseases that must be prevented. He believed that vaccinating other diseases is one of the factors causing our animals to be less resistant to those diseases.

There is a cost to restoring hardiness and vigor. Culling rates will increase for a time, average weaning weights will go down and during the transition period the savings on input costs may not cover the lost revenue resulting from lower performance. Would the advantage of having adapted animals that thrive without inputs be worth it? That's a question only my sister can answer for her operation. It's a question only you can answer for yours.

> We protect our animals from cold, heat, drought, too much rain, parasites, rough terrain, predators, poor quality feed and many other problems. The result is that we have created animals that need protection.

The Case Against Genetics

An article in a popular industry magazine claimed, "... given the multiple challenges you face that are beyond your control—drought, rising feed and fuel costs, escalating land values—genetic selection may be the single most important component of your operation that you control." If anyone out there believes that, please explain it to me, because I think genetics is WAY down the list of critical factors on which we, as business owners, need to focus. This really isn't a case against genetics. It is an argument for other things first.

What comes first? If you own a ranch and profit is one of your goals, start with the land, not the animals. Ranch land is worth a lot of money these days, but only a fraction of its value is tied to its potential for agricultural production. Capitalizing or concessionizing ranch resources may make a six- or even seven-figure difference to your bottom line. It's unlikely you'll get that kind of return from evaluating EPDs (Expected Progeny Differences).

Next? Some places are better suited to growing stock than breeding stock. Cow/calf enterprises on irrigated pasture usually aren't as profitable as stocker or heifer development enterprises could be on that same forage.

> It doesn't matter what breed of cow you have or how good a bull you use if you ought not have cows!

It'd be a good idea to make sure we have the right enterprise mix before we get too worried about the genetic makeup of the animals in that enterprise.

And there's more. Assuming a cow/calf enterprise is a good fit to our resource, let's determine *how* it fits. We would be well served to make sure our production schedule matches the forage cycle. In the Great Plains, winter calving (February–April) might produce a big calf but usually requires winter feeding and all of the overhead costs that go along with that. Spring calving

(May–June) may mean smaller calves, but often means less cost. The type of cow ideally suited to winter calving is unlikely to also be ideally suited for a low-cost summer program. Before we worry about breed and body type and start picking bulls and replacement heifers, wouldn't it be best to know which production strategy produces the highest margin, with the lowest overheads, and provides the most protection from risk (severe winters, drought, etc.)?

Since I brought it up, what about those heifers? I've already challenged the notions that we have to raise our own and that replacements have to be heifers. Our replacement strategy has as much or more impact on our profitability than the type of heifer we choose. The cost of raising them usually exceeds the economic value we get from controlling our genetics.

This is not to say that genetics aren't important. Having animals selected for and adapted to the environment and production schedule is important. But the magazine article is wrong in suggesting that it is the "single most important" thing that you control.

What really set me off as I read the article is the way it portrayed us as victims. It implied that we are victims of drought, rising feed and fuel costs and other externalities. I don't mean to diminish the challenges we face when input costs rise faster than cattle prices, or the economic and emotional toll we pay in drought, but the fact is that some of us weather the storm (or lack thereof) better than others. It's true that none of us individually dictates the cost of feed or fuel, or can make it rain. But our choice of enterprises and the way we structure those enterprises has everything to do with our exposure to the risk of drought, our need for feed and fuel and just about any other external factor you can name. Those decisions trump the economic impact of genetics. It doesn't matter what breed of cow you have or how good a bull you use if you ought not have cows!

The Search for the Perfect Cow

I like the way Glenn Barlow thinks about cows. Glenn has applied many of the principles we've discussed in this chapter to his ranch. He shifted the calving season from March and April and now uses a 45-day calving period starting in June. I asked him, if he could go back in time and make the shift again, would he do it the same way? He said no. He'd still have his cows calve in June, but he said that he'd change the way he made the transition. Rather than shift a productive herd selected for spring calving to a new production schedule, he thought it would have been better to sell that herd and replace them with other people's late-calving cows. Culled late calvers would be inexpensive because they didn't fit someone else's program, but they would already be in synch with Glenn's.

What about health and handling problems? Glenn said that there are simple tactics to minimize those. There might be a downside to that strategy ... they might have had to pay some capital gains tax, selling a valuable herd and replacing it with animals that didn't cost so much, but that's a good problem.

Glenn said that he's changed his thinking about how well his herd fits his resources. At one time he felt the cattle were well adapted to the ranch. That was

> "I don't want to work for these cows. They're supposed to be working for me."
> *Glenn Barlow*

the result of years of careful selection. But those cows had to be fed hay and receive the inputs used in conventional ranching to maintain production.

Glenn told me that he's working toward developing a herd that is *really* adapted. He sees a cow that's wide with a deep body but significantly smaller in overall size than most of the cows in the area. He thought she'd be better able to maintain body condition year-round under range conditions. She probably wouldn't produce a lot of milk. She would wean a live calf every year, carrying that calf by her side for 10 months without substitute feeding for either the cow or the calf through the winter. Glenn thought his cows should be red or buckskin in color. Last summer he used a laser thermometer to measure the temperature on the back of his cows. The ambient temperature was 95°F, but the surface temperature of the black cows ranged from 138 to 142°F. The temperature of the red cows was only 118°F.

Glenn's ranch has been in a severe drought for the past couple of years. He told me that the drought gave him the opportunity to accelerate progress toward creating his herd of adapted cows. Because carrying capacity was down, he culled very heavily, selling the cows least suited to his management program.

When Glenn achieves the herd that fits his ranch resources, he said the roles on the ranch will be completely reversed. He will no longer be working for the cows. The cows will be working for him.

2. Happy Families

Hard Work and Harmony

Ranching is not just about land, grass, cows and money. It is about our families, our employees, the people we buy from and the people we sell too. It is also about our own relationship to our ranch. Is ranching our job or our business, our hobby or our profession?

Do You Own a Business or a Job?

- Amateurs Pay to Play

- You Won't Win by Playing Not to Lose

- You Might Own Your Job If ...

- Chicken and Egg Syndrome

- Prime Time for Prime Work

Amateurs Pay to Play

In sports you are either a professional athlete or an amateur athlete. The amateurs pay to play. The professionals get paid to play. Amateurs play for the love of the game. Professionals play for money, but that doesn't mean they love the game any less. In fact, that could be a reason for loving it even more.

There are two types of ranchers: professionals and amateurs. Professionals get paid to ranch. Amateurs pay to ranch. Most amateurs have a deep love of the land and/or livestock. So do the professionals.

Professional versus amateur is more a function of attitude and commitment than scale. Scale is important in any business, but there are many 1,000-plus cow ranches that are subsidized with off-farm income and unpaid family labor. They are amateurs and they pay to play.

In contrast, there are many smaller part-time professional ranchers who are highly profitable. One south Texas *Ranching For Profit School* alumnus refers to his 500-cow outfit as his *weekend job*. After all, no one ever said that ranching has to be a full-time business.

Speaking to the Montana Stockgrowers Association several years ago, I referred to ranching as a challenging *profession*. A woman came up to me during a break and asked, "Do you really think ranching is a profession? I've never heard anyone else call it that."

Is the distinction really all that important? You tell me. Won't people who believe ranching is a profession and see themselves as professionals do things much differently than someone who believes otherwise? Whether it is a profession and you are a professional is entirely up to you.

Someone with 50 cows might think, "Someday, when I get bigger, I will become a professional rancher." The problem is that it is unlikely that they will grow their operation in any meaningful way *unless* they treat the ranch as a business and ranching as their profession.

In *The E-Myph Revisited*, Michael Gerber relates a story about Tom Watson, the founder of IBM. He's quotes Watson as saying, "I realized that for IBM to become a great company it would have to act like a great company long before it ever became one." A similar truth can be said of becoming a professional rancher. In order to become one, you have to be one ... now.

You might think, "But that's IBM. IBM is a great business ... a great big business." But size is not the point. Any ranch that improves the health of the land, produces a profit, provides opportunities for family members and achieves the other things *you* want to achieve is a great business. Watson's point was your ranch won't become a great business unless you act as though it already is a great business.

> Amateurs pay to ranch.
> Professionals get paid to ranch.

You Won't Win by Playing Not to Lose

It's the fourth quarter and your team is up by three touch-downs. The coaches deviate from the game plan. With the win all but assured, they start playing not to lose. The play calling gets conservative and they shift to their "prevent" defense.

Why don't they start the game in prevent defense? Any football fan can tell you that it's because you don't win by playing not to lose. Most ranchers manage their ranches as though they were playing not to lose.

I often start conversations with *Ranching For Profit School* participants by asking, "What do you want?" Many participants respond by telling me what they don't want. If I ask, "What would you like to see financially?" they often say, "I'd like to be debt free." Their focus is on a problem, namely, too much debt. If they looked a little deeper they might find that what they really want is financial security. They might also realize that some debt on some things at some times might actually be a tool that could help them achieve financial security faster. Focusing on the problem can actually perpetuate the problem. Focusing on the problem is like playing not to lose.

Consider a weedy pasture. We tend to focus on the problem and look for ways to kill the weeds. I once heard Allan Savory say, "As long as you spray weeds, you'll have weeds to spray." By focusing on killing weeds (the problem), we tend to do things that increase capping and compaction, worsen the water cycle and reduce biodiversity. That's like putting a welcome mat out for more weeds. Strategies that improve the health of your pastures are different from the methods we use to eradicate weeds. By focusing on what we want, a healthy grassland, weed problems often solve themselves. Besides, doesn't a healthy pasture full of palatable, nutritious forage for our animals sound more appealing than one free of weeds?

This is more than semantics and motivational gobbledygook. Most people spend their lives solving problems. It's like a never-ending game of "whack-a-mole." Once we get on top of one problem, another pops up. Our focus is on keeping bad things from happening. That's expensive and exhausting.

Rather than focusing on what you *don't* want, how would it feel to focus on what you *do* want? What if rather than killing the weeds, we focused on growing grass? What if instead of avoiding debt, we implemented a plan to create a secure financial future? What if instead of avoiding conflict, we worked on creating an environment in which all voices were listened to with respect?

At a recent workshop in Colorado, someone told me that her goal was to stop the arguing in her family. Again, the focus was on what she wanted to prevent, not on what she wanted to create. I wondered aloud if it might be more constructive to learn how to argue so that everyone's voice was heard and considered in decisions. Discussing the issues effectively so that everyone's voice is heard will likely lead to better decisions and more support for those decisions. I suggested that a more powerful vision might be a united family.

> "You don't get harmony when everyone sings the same note."
> Doug Floyd

If you created a shared vision of the future, wouldn't making progress toward achieving it be more exhilarating than exhausting? Keeping bad things from happening saps our energy. Making progress toward creating good things energizes us. When one focuses on the vision, many of the problems we spent so much time addressing simply slip away.

Managing for what you want is playing to win. Managing against the things you don't want is playing not to lose. Which way do you want to play?

You Might Own Your Job If ...

It's been said that when you are self-employed, you don't really own a business, you own a job. In his book *Cash Flow Quadrant*, Robert Kiyosaki says that people who own a business can leave for a year, and when they come back, they will find the operation working even better than when they left. If you can't leave, or if things would fall apart if you did, according to Kiyosaki you don't own a business, you own a job.

You might think that Kiyosaki's criterion doesn't apply to ranching. Perhaps you are right. Let's change it to a month or even a week. A lot of people tell me that they'd like to attend *The Ranching For Profit School* but can't because they can't get away from the ranch for a week. A week! If that's the case, maybe they don't own their job, perhaps their job owns them!

Most ranches resemble a collection of assets and a bunch of jobs more than they do a real business. Whether you accept Kiyosaki's rule of one year, or my watered down criterion of a month or even a week, there are several other things to consider:

1. Do you react to new ideas that would increase your profit by thinking, "When will I find the time to do that?" If you do, you own a job, and the last thing you need is another one. A business owner would think, "How can I get someone to make that happen?"

2. If you sold the ranch, would you only be selling a collection of assets? If you were selling a business, in addition to the assets you would be selling documented production, sales, finance and management systems that show how to use those assets to serve customers, create positive cash flow and produce a profit.

3. Does your ranch have a purpose beyond profit,

> Is your ranch a business, or is it a collection of assets and a bunch of jobs?

and does it serve someone other than you and your family? The primary purpose of a business is to serve a customer. Only by serving a customer can a business make a profit and serve the owner. Interestingly, when our focus shifts from ourselves to our customers, we get better results for ourselves.

4. Does $5,000 per year seem like a lot to spend on professional development? It is a lot to spend on doing your job better, but it's a drop in the bucket to invest in building a better business.

5. Have you ever said, "I really ought to manage this as *though* it was a business?" This phrase acknowledges that your ranch isn't really a business. We can act *as though* it is a business for a while, but it isn't sustainable to pretend.

6. Does your ranch make an economic profit? Without the subsidies that most ranchers use to survive (e.g., off-farm income, inherited wealth, working for less than it would cost to replace yourself), would your ranch be able to cover all of its costs and have a healthy return on investment? If it isn't profitable, it isn't sustainable. In fact, it isn't even a business. It's a hobby. Most ranches are very expensive hobbies.

We talk about ranching as though we have to choose between living the ranching lifestyle *or* running a ranching business. It is a false choice. Transforming the ranch into a business tends to improve the quality of life. Nebraska rancher and *Ranching For Profit School* alumnus Derek Schwanebeck put it this way: "When we focused on our life, all we did was work our butts off. When we focused on our business, our life got so much better."

• • •

After reading a *ProfitTips* posting on this topic, a reader asked how someone could go about "changing the operation so that they become business owners."

That's a great question. Most people look for change "out there," but this change must start within us. Making the transition from self-employed to business owner requires a fundamental paradigm shift. It is more about how we think and feel than what we do.

If we aren't currently getting the results we want financially and personally, we have to start doing things differently. Intellectually we know that the jobs involved in raising and marketing livestock are different than the jobs required to run a successful business that raises and markets livestock. But the barrier to transforming our ranches into successful businesses is this: even if we recognize the ranch is a business, we don't see ourselves as business men and women. We see ranching as our job and our ranch as our place of work. The essential paradigm shift from being self-employed to being a business owner begins with seeing our ranch as our business and ourselves as business men and women.

Chicken and Egg Syndrome

Sam sent me an email to say, "Since the *Ranching For Profit School*, I have been more enthusiastic about ranching than I have been in 15 years. I have never had as many tools in my hands to create success."

I find it rewarding, but not surprising, to receive comments like this. Hundreds of ranchers tell us that the school has been a transformational experience for them. Their good experiences make it harder to read emails like this one from a young couple who asked for information about our programs. They wrote, "Unfortunately, we can't make it to the class. It's very hard to stay away from the farm for more than two days, as we don't have employees or anyone to do our chores."

If someone can't leave the farm for more than two days, the farm isn't a business. It is a collection of jobs, probably very low paying jobs with no days off and no vacation. I've seen a lot of smart, talented young people in the same situation, wasting years of their lives, years they will never have back, treating life as though it was something that was going to happen later. Sometimes it seems as though they think that farming and ranching means they have to take a vow of poverty and an oath to work, or at least be on call 24/7/365.

It is great to be young, smart and full of energy, but it can also work to our disadvantage. When we are young, smart and full of energy, we tend to build businesses that require someone who is young, smart and full of energy. When we get a little older and have kids in school, 4-H, FFA and sports, we may find ourselves trapped. It is as though we painted ourselves into a corner and the paint never dries. The

> Rather than build a business that requires youth, brains and energy, we'd be better off to build one that would work even if we were old, dumb and lazy.

93

ranch, which is actually a collection of jobs more than a business, requires someone young, smart and full of energy, but we aren't as young and we feel worn out physically, mentally and emotionally.

Rather than supporting our life, too often we find our life is spent supporting the ranch. Rather than adding to our life, it takes away from our life. It doesn't have to be that way.

The young couple who said they can't get away for more than two days believe they are stuck in the classic chicken and egg syndrome: unless they do something different than what they've been doing, nothing will ever change, but they can't take the time to learn something new *until* things change. But this isn't a case of which comes first, the chicken or the egg. What comes first is learning a new way to do things.

An old adage tells us, "If you really want to do something, you can always find a way, but if you don't really want to do it, you can always find an excuse." Rather than pay someone to do their $10-per-hour jobs for a week so they can focus on the $100-per-hour and $1,000-per-hour work, they choose to be stuck.

People generally need two things to embrace change. First, they have to feel enough pain to be motivated to move. Perhaps this young couple hasn't reached that threshold yet. Sadly, farmers and ranchers tend to have a high pain threshold. By the time the status quo becomes intolerable, they may have run out of time, energy, money and options.

The second thing people need in order to embrace change is the belief that things can be better. I wonder if the young couple stuck on the ranch believe that it is possible for things to be different. If they don't believe the

A sustainable business can not rely on unsustainable effort.

situation can improve it would be a waste of time, energy and money to try.

Don't treat life as though it is something that is going to happen later. A sustainable business cannot rely on unsustainable effort. Tom Lasater once said, "The cattle business is a very simple business. The complicated part is to keep it simple." Take Tom's advice to heart. Use your enthusiasm, brains and energy to create a business that would work for someone old, dumb and lazy.

Prime Time for Prime Work

On every ranch there are at least two kinds of work: $10-per-hour jobs and $100-per-hour jobs. The $10-per-hour jobs include mending fence, feeding cows and other chores. We call the $10-per-hour jobs WITB, which stands for *Working In The Business*. The $100-per-hour work, which we call WOTB for *Working On The Business*, involves establishing long-range goals and making plans to reach them. It includes creating a management succession plan, a drought plan, a marketing plan ... you get the idea. There are so many $10-per-hour jobs that need to be done on every ranch that it isn't surprising that most of our time is spent on WITB.

Just as there are two kinds of work on a ranch, we also have two kinds of time. We have time when we are worth $100 per hour and time when we are worth only $10 per hour. For most of us, the $100-per-hour time comes first thing in the morning. What do most of us do in our $100-per-hour time? We do our $10-per-hour work. If we ever get to the $100-per-hour jobs, it is usually after we are worn out from a day of WITB and are worth only $10 per hour, if that.

At *The Ranching For Profit School* we suggest that alumni take two mornings a week for WOTB. By doing their $100-per-hour work in their $100-per-hour time, they increase their effectiveness. That often dramatically reduces the time needed for the $10-per-hour jobs.

Northern California rancher Andy McBride once said, "When I first went to *The Ranching For Profit School*, I didn't know where I would find the time to do the planning. Once I started the planning, I realized I was spending 80% of my time fixing equipment I didn't even need."

It doesn't do any good to work hard if you are working on the wrong things. My Australian colleagues put it this way, "Head down, bum up, running like hell, getting nowhere!"

Andy is in good company. Once they make time for WOTB, many *Ranching For Profit School* alumni discover they are spending time and energy doing things that don't need to be done.

The key is to take the time to work *on* your business. Two mornings a week of WOTB will reduce your overall workload, increase the value of your $10-per-hour time and ensure that time and energy is taking you in the right direction. Prime time for prime work.

> Every ranch has $10-per-hour jobs and $100-per-hour jobs.
> Each of us has $10-per-hour time and $100-per-hour time.
> We need to do our $100-per-hour jobs in our $100-per-hour time.

Employee Compensation and Accountability

- A Working Paradigm

- Money May Not Make People Happy, but Happy People Make Money

- Pay Me Now or Pay Me Later

- *They* Need to be Held Accountable

- Trust but Verify

A Working Paradigm

Hiring a cowboy for $25,000 per year actually costs closer to $60,000. Payroll taxes, health insurance, vehicle costs, housing, horses, dogs, and all the other costs associated with hiring and supporting an employee add up fast. That's a lot of money, especially considering the average ranch produces a gross product of only $80,000 per employee. (Gross product is a measure of the total value produced by an enterprise or a business.) Subtract the $60,000 it takes to support an employee from the gross product he or she produced, and you are left with less than $20,000 to pay the rent, the interest on the cow loan, the feed bill and all other expenses. What's left after that is profit. If there's nothing left, you aren't alone. This is why we work for free on the ranch and hold off-farm jobs to support our ranching habit.

To calculate the gross product per full time employees (FTE) for your ranch, follow these three simple steps:

1. Calculate your gross product using this formula:

    Closing Inventory Value
    + Sales
    − Purchases (inventory expansion or replacement)
    − Opening Inventory Value
    _____
    Gross Product

2. Count up the total FTE's on your ranch, including unpaid or underpaid family labor.
3. Divide your gross product by the total FTE's. The result is the average gross product produced per employee.

I recently led a workshop in which I showed participants how to use benchmarks to identify profit drivers and pinpoint weaknesses in their ranches. The benchmarks were created by taking actual data from highly profitable ranch businesses in our *Executive Link* program. The benchmark for gross product per

FTE is $200,000. In other words, in benchmark businesses the average employee produces about $200,000 of economic value.

When I shared this benchmark, I heard a young rancher in the second row whisper to his friend, "Man, I wouldn't want to do that." I wondered, "Why wouldn't he want to create $200,000 of value?" I think I know the answer.

Gross Product/FTE

Typical Ranch ≈ $80,000

Benchmark Ranch ≥ $200,000

When I was young, if I asked my parents for money, they would have given me some extra chores or told me to ask the neighbor for a job to earn it. Most of us learn this lesson at a young age: *you have to work to make money.* The corollary is: *to make more money, you have to do more work.* I'm sure the young rancher grew up with the same influence. If his ranch was like most of his neighbors', he probably imagined that to produce two-and-a-half times the value (increasing gross product from $80,000 to $200,000), he'd have to do two-and-a-half times as much work. Already working sunup to sundown, that would be impossible.

But dramatically increasing the gross product per FTE doesn't usually require working longer or harder. It requires that we work smarter. *Ranching for Profit School* alumnus Derek Schwanebeck summed it up well when he said, "We work our brains way harder than we work our bodies these days." Rather than working to support their ranches, Derek and other alumni have built ranches that work to support them.

Significant increases in gross product per FTE come from working our brains harder than our bodies.

It is usually pretty easy to tell if you are on a place where the gross product per FTE is high. It's the place where people are smiling. They usually have more fun and don't work as long and hard as people producing less value.

Ask most ranchers what gives them satisfaction from their work, and they'll usually lead the list with "accomplishing something" or "seeing results." Who do you think feels more satisfaction, someone who produced $80,000 worth of results or someone who produced $200,000 of results? Money may not make people happy, but happy people make money.

Money May Not Make People Happy, but Happy People Make Money

Most of us hire people to work. We write job descriptions describing the work we want employees to do. But what people do and how long or hard they work is not important. It is only the means to the end. The end is the *results* they produce.

As an employer you would be well served to start thinking about work this way, because the people you employ already do! In survey after survey, workers report that *the* thing that motivates them more than anything else is *achievement*. Perhaps it is time we stopped calling them *workers* and started calling them *achievers*. Maybe we ought to stop writing *job descriptions* and start writing *achievement descriptions*.

The technical term for an achievement description is an *effectiveness area*. While job descriptions describe what we expect an employee to do, effectiveness areas describe the results an employee is expected to produce. More precisely, effectiveness areas describe an employee's responsibilities. Once we've defined and assigned an effectiveness area to an employee, we establish a target against which we can measure the results.

Searching the internet for job openings on ranches I found this posting:

Wanted: Ranch Hand
Duties include all aspects of farm and ranch work including:
- working with cows (calving, sorting, hauling, weaning, etc.)
- fixing fence and tanks and pipelines
- driving truck and operating heavy machinery (seeder, tractors, balers, haybine).

Mechanical and welding experience is also helpful.

This position announcement describes what they want the person to do. There isn't one word about the results they want the employee to achieve. If we were to rewrite this using effectiveness areas, it might read:

Wanted: Ranch Hand
Responsibilities include:
- Livestock production
- Facilities maintenance
- Enterprise gross margin.

For each of these effectiveness areas we'd assign a measurable target. For example, for the Livestock Production effectiveness area we could set a weaning rate target of ≥90% or a rate of gain target of two pounds per day.

Our employee would be asked to develop (or help us develop) a plan showing how to produce the results and meet the target. This process gives us a way to objectively measure performance and hold employees accountable for producing results.

That may sound like a lot to expect from an employee. That's okay. I just looked through a website connecting people who are looking for ranch work with ranches looking for workers. The job seekers outnumbered the job openings by more than two to one. Employers can be choosy. And if you are looking for a job, what better way to distinguish yourself from the pack than to show a prospective employer the results you can produce.

My good friend and colleague Roger Ingram emailed me a resume he saw posted online by someone who was looking for a ranch management position. The person posting the resume used bullet points to list his extensive experience. The job seeker included things like having owned and operated a cow/calf and stocker outfit in Wyoming, having raised replacement heifers in Nebraska, having managed a moderate-sized feedlot and having worked with agency personnel and bankers.

That all sounds like good experience, but as Roger pointed out, the resume would have been even more impressive if the focus was not on what the applicant had done, but on what he had achieved. Roger offered the following suggestions. What if the job seeker had written:

- Increased the gross margin by $200/Standard Animal Unit by eliminating substitute feeding.
- Used low-stress livestock handling skills to run more cows/employee, increasing the gross product from $90,000/FTE to $150,000/FTE.
- Lowered the overhead ratio from 65% to 45%.
- Increased the number of total stock days grazed by 35% using cell grazing.
- Developed 15 additional livestock water points.
- Increased ground cover by 35%.
- Facilitated the development of a drought plan.

Which resume is more impressive to you?

> Don't hire people to work. Hire them to produce results.

The only result the job seeker mentioned in his lengthy resume was that they had typically weaned a 94–96% calf crop. But if this weaning percentage was the result of conventional winter feeding practices (e.g., feeding 2–3 tons of hay per cow), it may be that a 90% weaning percentage would be more profitable. In fact, after reading Roger's suggested outcomes, I started wondering, did the cow/calf operation in Wyoming go broke? Was the replacement heifer operation in Nebraska a money pit?

The challenge of using effectiveness areas is not setting the bar high for *employees*; it is setting the bar high for employers. To use effectiveness areas, employers need to be clear on the results they need to run a successful business.

A friend recently told me of an experience he'd gone through finding a good employee. It took him a long time. After a long day working together, he asked his new man, "Do you know how long it's taken me to find a good employee?" Without a moment's hesitation the new employee responded, "I'll bet it wasn't nearly as long as it's taken me to find a good boss."

Don't hire people to work. Hire them to produce results.

Pay Me Now or Pay Me Later

I am not an advice columnist, but I do get my share of *Dear Dave* letters and emails. Here's a *Dear Dave* inquiry I received recently:

Dear Dave,

We have a problem. Our ranch manager is a family member but does not have equity in the ranch. This year, because of the drought, we received a government crop insurance payment and we made a big profit. The manager says we got the payment, and therefore the profit, due to his skill in applying for the insurance program. In addition to his annual salary of $60,000, he is demanding a 5% annual profit share. Is this fair? Please advise.

Want To Be Fair

Dear Want To Be Fair,

So he wants a share of the profit. Would your business have made a profit had there not been a drought, or are you hoping for a drought every year? If you make a loss will he expect you to take a portion of the loss out of his paycheck? I don't know what people in your area are getting paid, but in my opinion a ranch manager paid $60K per year isn't in much of a position to "demand" anything. That's pretty good compensation relative to what other managers get ... and I don't respond well to "demands." If the demands persist, politely listen, then show him the door and wish him luck finding work in this economy. On the other hand, if the employee approached me with concerns about his compensation, I'd listen to understand the concerns and make every effort to work out a fair arrangement.

Dave

This letter underscores the importance of having a formal written policy about employing family members. Family members ought to be held to the same standards to which you would hold non-family employees. But the more immediate issue in the letter has to do with compensation, so I told *Want To Be Fair* that there are three possible elements to a compensation plan:

Salary and benefits pay for the work

People need to be paid enough so that they focus on work, not on how they are going to put food on the table for their families. Beyond that, money isn't very motivating.

Employees may not recognize the value of the benefits they receive. I recommend making a list of all of the perks (vehicle, housing, side of beef, hunting, etc.) that each person gets. Document the value of each of those things. This is not intended to lay a guilt trip on anyone. It is simply to make the true value of the compensation package clear.

Bonuses reward achievement

Bonuses reward employees for their achievement. If you choose to use a bonus, make sure that it is tied to achievement of individual goals *and* team goals. Set a minimum target that has to be achieved for the bonus to kick in. After all, people ought to be expected to produce some minimum result. They should not get a bonus for ordinary performance.

As a rule of thumb, set the bar high and make the bonus big. Whatever the bonus is based on (e.g., profit, gross margin), you need to be perfectly clear on how it is going to be measured.

Money is not a very effective motivator. If you don't pay someone enough they won't like it. But if you pay someone more than they are worth, it is unlikely to motivate them to accomplish more. When bonuses work (and they often backfire), it's not the money as much as the recognition for achievement the money represents that makes it work.

Are there non-cash rewards that might mean more to your employees than money? Which would be remembered longer, a $5,000 cash bonus or a week for two at the National Finals Rodeo in Las Vegas with air fare, lodging and $500 spending money?

> "You can buy someone's hands, but you can't buy their mind, and that's where their creativity comes from. Nor can you buy their heart, and that's where their loyalty comes from."
>
> *Stan Parsons*

At Ranch Management Consultants we don't pay a monetary bonus. Instead we often buy a gift (usually a gift certificate to an employee's favorite restaurant) to recognize special achievement. We also pay a profit share. If the company does well, we like to share the success with the people who helped create it, whether they had a direct hand in it or not. The profit share is not used as a tool to motivate our staff. Instead we use it to reinforce that we are all part of the RMC team.

Participate in growth

You may want to reward people who are going to contribute to the long-term growth of your business with an equity position. Some businesses use "phantom shares" to compensate key long-term employees with equity. The employees get a share of the increase in equity that occurs during their tenure. When employment is terminated, the shares are purchased back by the company.

Growth participation is one way of establishing a retirement program for long-term employees ... but again, you need to be able to buy them out when they leave.

Don Jonovic of Family Business Management Services, who first introduced me to this tool, says that using phantom shares tends to keep good people around longer but also makes it harder to get rid of someone should things turn south. That's why, before you do something like this, you need to be pretty darn sure you have the right person. It would be a good idea to establish a vesting period of at least three to five years before any growth participation becomes part of an employee's compensation.

Regardless of the compensation package, you need to determine what competent managers are paid for similar responsibilities in your region. Check with your local extension folks to see if they have data on salaries for people doing comparable work. I suggest you share that information with the employee. Then, set some objective criteria to define competence, and measure the employee's performance relative to those standards regularly (e.g., semi-annually). Once you've measured the performance, you must review it with the employee in a formal performance review. Keep in mind this is not an evaluation of the employee. It is an evaluation of the employee's *performance*. There's a big difference.

I ended my letter to *Want To Be Fair* by suggesting that while the manager is demanding more money, there may be a deeper issue. I wonder if he is really demanding respect or appreciation. Stan Parsons once told me, "You can buy someone's hands, but you can't buy their mind, and that's where their creativity comes from. Nor can you buy their heart, and that's where their loyalty comes from." Paying more for his hands doesn't mean you'll get his mind or his heart.

They Need to be Held Accountable

According to Michael Gerber in *The E-Myth Revisited*, when you are self-employed you work for a lunatic. It has nothing to do with intelligence or how hard we work. Most of us are plenty smart and work hard enough. The problem is we work on the things we enjoy and the things we are good at, the $10-per-hour jobs, while leaving $100- and $1,000-per-hour jobs undone. No one holds us accountable.

I've had conversations with several members of ranching families in which a family member will say something like, "We talk about the plan and are assured that it will be implemented, but there's no follow-through. We need a way of holding *insert name here* accountable."

I often suggest the family shareholders actually do what their bylaws say they do, and that's have board meetings where strategy is discussed, goals are set, performance is evaluated relative to those goals and people are held accountable. In many cases, it is smart to have trusted, non-family members who understand business on your board.

"That's great," they say. But when I ask, "What targets would *you* be accountable for?" the optimistic smile turns into a deer-in-the-headlights stare. We want others to be held accountable, but we neither want to be the ones to hold them accountable nor do we want to be accountable to someone else. Some of us seem to like working for a lunatic.

The multi-generational ranching lifestyle eventually leads to a wreck unless we make the distinction between our family and our family business. We need professional management. Growing up with one-half of your DNA

> The multi-generational ranching lifestyle eventually leads to a wreck unless we make the distinction between our family and our family business.

does not predispose your children to managerial excellence. If they are going to run the business, they need to become professional managers. Without professional management, sooner or later the romanticized lifestyle we dream about will become a nightmare.

Trust but Verify

I joke that it is easier to run the neighbor's ranch and solve someone else's problems than our own. But it's no joke. Things that are invisible to us are often obvious to others. Sometimes we can't see the obstacles that stand in the way of our success. The most challenging, and sadly all-too-common, obstacles are dysfunctional relationships between family members. It is why ranches don't make it from one generation to another and why, for some, the ranching "lifestyle" is a lifestyle of resentment and misery.

I've met with ranching families who are so dysfunctional they won't even talk to one another. In one case, a family member whose share in the ranch was worth over $10 million harbored so much ill will against the others that he wouldn't even come to a meeting that I was asked to facilitate to discuss the future of the ranch. I spent several hours on the phone with him prior to the meeting listening to his pain. When I met with the other family members I insisted that they address the question, "How do you run a business when one of the largest shareholders feels so much resentment that he won't participate in board meetings and even threatens to sue the others?"

After a surprisingly productive meeting, I summarized the conclusions I intended to include in my report. Then I told them that since the business was my client and the business is owned by all of them, including the family member who wouldn't participate, I planned to send my report to *all* the shareholders. I asked, "How do you feel about that?" Their answer could have come from an elementary school playground: "He wasn't here to give us his input, so I don't want to share ours!" It would be comical if it wasn't so sad.

The resentment these family members, now in their 60's, carry with them infects everything they do. It began growing

> "Resentment is like taking poison and waiting for the other person to die."
>
> *Malachy McCourt*

when they were kids, and for 50 years no one has been willing or able to apologize or forgive. Unfortunately, they have lots of company. Many of us find some strange kind of validation in blaming each other. But holding on to that resentment harms us more than it harms anyone else. The resentment kills us emotionally and spiritually, and the stress kills us physically. If we could only let go. If only.

In our *7 Habits of Highly Effective People* class we use the metaphor of the "emotional bank account." We make deposits by keeping commitments and by helping one another. We make withdrawals when we do hurtful things and break promises. Some relationships are so severely overdrawn they will never have a positive balance unless someone forgives the debt. But sometimes we act as though we'd rather carry the debt than let an overdrawn family member even try to repay it. We tend to wear our scars like a badge of honor so everyone can see how we've been hurt.

The reasons we won't forgive and can't forget are many and complex, but at the foundation of all of them is the erosion of trust. We need to work on our overdrawn relationships to rebuild trust, but we also need to separate family relationship issues from the issues critical to running a successful business. As suggested in the best-selling book on negotiation *Getting to Yes*, we need to separate the people issues from the business issues.

But how do you work through business issues when there is no trust? In *Getting to Yes*, Roger Fisher and William Ury explain that trust doesn't have to be an issue. A great example of this principle was summed up by Ronald Regan referring to a nuclear arms treaty being negotiated with the Soviet Union. He said, "Trust, but verify." By agreeing on objective standards by which performance will be measured, trust is not the issue, performance is.

Stories From the ~~Trenches~~ Ranches

- A Frustrated Employee

- Budgeting Time and Money

- The Freedom of My Chains

- Selling Change

- Separating the Land Business from the Livestock Business

- Fool Me Once

A Frustrated Employee

One evening after class at a *Ranching For Profit School* in Montana, a young couple came to me expressing frustration about their situation. In that day's session they'd learned how to use cell grazing to increase the health and productivity of the ranch while cutting input costs. The day before they'd learned how to project cash flow, enterprise gross margins and profit or loss. The day before that they'd learned a method for getting everyone on the same page and working together as a team. They saw how defining roles and setting performance targets could be used to produce better results and hold people accountable.

In spite of all that (or maybe because of it), the stress they felt was palpable. They said they knew that the things they were learning could dramatically improve the situation on the ranch. They were frustrated because they were certain they would only be able to implement a fraction of what they were learning. They didn't have the authority to make the changes they wanted to make.

I'd like to see all of our alumni implementing all of the things they learn—that's why we offer *Executive Link* as a support program to guide them in applying *Ranching For Profit School* concepts. Of course, the couple expressing frustration wouldn't be the ones to decide if the ranch participated in *Executive Link*. So what could they do?

I suggested they not worry about things they could do nothing about and focus only on the things that were within their control. "But we don't have any control," they protested.

> Rather than worrying about the things you can't control, how would things change if you focused on the things you can control?

"Really? You don't have *any* control?" I asked. "Could you use the tools we discussed today to create a proposal for the owners that included a budget, a marketing plan and performance targets? Could you include an estimate of the capital these changes will require and run projections on best- and worst-case scenarios?" You should have seen their expressions change. Their frustration and tension were replaced with genuine excitement. Suddenly they felt empowered and in control. I have no doubt they'll create a darn good proposal. Even so, I suggested that rather than count on the plan being accepted, they consider submitting it as a draft and asking the owners for their input.

Things We Can't Do Anything About	Things We Can Do Something About
Cattle prices	Developing alternative markets
Weather	Selecting enterprises and production strategies compatible with the environment
Other people's reaction to our proposal	The content of our proposal and the way we present it

Too often we waste time and emotional energy frustrated by things beyond our control. Worse, in that wasted time lie the seeds of resentment and depression. When those seeds grow, they get tangled up with everything we do and every relationship we have.

Rather than focusing on things we can't control, what if we took that time to identify the things we actually can do something about? What a difference it would make if we focused on just those things.

Budgeting Time and Money

A *Ranching For Profit School* alumnus contacted me last week asking for help. He said that his mother was feeling stressed about a plan they had created at a recent WOTB (Working On The Business) meeting. She was especially worried about the debt and the workload assigned to him and his father.

I suggested he have a conversation with his mother to discuss her concerns. But I also recommended he do his homework. He should prepare a cash flow to show how the debt will be managed and a work flow to show how labor will be allocated in the months ahead.

Too often we forget that a cash flow isn't just a budget, it is a plan. It shows how much income you expect and when you expect it. It shows what you plan to spend and when you plan to spend it. It shows periods of cash surpluses and deficits and provides a vehicle to show how you'll manage through those periods. I suggested he use it to show his mother when the income will come in, how debt will be serviced and how the business's obligations will be met. He should run through some scenarios with her. For example, he may think his budget assumptions are realistic, but what if cattle prices tank or if it doesn't rain? I suggested that he project a cash flow forecast that shows how they could cope with these and other worrisome scenarios. If he doesn't have a contingency plan, then it is time for a WOTB meeting to make one.

> The cash flow is a summary of the year's operating plan written in dollars.

Just as you can (and should) budget your money, you can (and should) also budget your time. I recommend drawing a week-by-week bar graph showing the blocks of time that will be required for various tasks through the year. I suggested the alumnus show the time required for routine maintenance, special projects, WOTB and personal priorities. If the graph shows more than 50 hours of WITB (Working In The Business) for more than a couple of weeks in a row, I suggested he take a hard look at his assumptions. Things always take longer than we think they will. Besides, there will always be unanticipated crises; this is ranching, after all. If the workload is too much, he will need to decide what he will do to lessen it (postpone a task, contract something out, hire temporary help, etc.).

There is only one big difference between planning the flow of cash in and out of your business and planning the flow of time. The amount of cash coming in and out is variable. The amount of time is fixed. We can do things to generate more cash and control our expenses. But we can't create more time; we can only control how we spend it. In either case, the critical issue is planning.

The Freedom of My Chains

There is a great line in a Kris Kristofferson song that goes, "Looking back and longing for the freedom of my chains ..." I love that line, "the freedom of my chains."

A couple from a multi-generation ranch attended a recent *Ranching For Profit School.* They told me they were frustrated that her parents shot down every new idea before it could even be considered. I started to tell them about the due diligence process we use in our *Executive Link* program to help people work through new ideas. Someone else in a similar situation who was sitting in on the conversation was skeptical. "Structure stifles creativity," he said. That can be true but, like the freedom offered by Kristofferson's chains, structure can also be liberating. By providing the security that we won't miss something and make a dumb decision, structure can free us to create and consider new ideas. See if you agree.

Have you ever proposed an idea only to have it shot down? Maybe it was a bad idea, but good or bad, most of the time our ideas don't get a fair hearing. In the court of ideas it is guilty until proven innocent. We are very comfortable showing why something is a bad idea. But once we make the negative case we rarely consider the positive. That safely preserves the status quo and sets us up to miss important opportunities.

If we had a process to protect us from making bad decisions we could feel safe in giving new ideas a fair hearing. This is why structure creates freedom. Knowing that all sides of an issue will be addressed before a decision is made makes it safe to explore those ideas.

> Knowing that all sides of an issue will be addressed gives people the security to explore possibilities they might otherwise resist.

The structure we use in *Executive Link* to explore new ideas consists of eight steps:

1. **Situation report**
   Include pertinent facts and figures without any spin. It is also important to identify things we don't know so we can fill in the gaps in our understanding.

2. **The proposal**
   The proposal should include gross margin projections, a cash flow forecast, an estimate of the capital required and the expected return on investment. How will it impact labor and the allocation of other resources? Like the situation report, the proposal should focus on facts and figures.

3. **The upside**
   Explore the positive aspects of the proposal. Identify all of the positive things that could happen as a result of implementing this idea. If the upside is big it will energize the process. If it isn't big enough, it isn't worth implementing and you don't need to continue this process.

4. **The downside**
   What are all of the possible negatives that could happen if this idea were implemented? Some people want to start with the negative. They will usually be satisfied to wait as long as they know their concerns will be heard. To make sure they know they've been heard, it is a good idea to repeat their comments (both positives and negatives) while writing them on a flip chart.

5. **Scoring**
   How big and how likely are the positives and the negatives?

6. **Alternatives**

   Create and explore ideas that could make the upside bigger and more likely and that could make the downside smaller and less likely.

7. **Emotions**

   Ask each person how she or he feels about the idea now that it has been explored. Ask what it is about the concept that is exciting or worrisome.

8. **Decision**

   Now that you've explored the idea, it is time to make a decision. If more information is needed, identify the unknowns that must be made known in order to make a decision. Assign each unknown to someone on the team and set a time when they will report their findings so a decision can be made.

Knowing that all sides of an issue will be addressed gives people the security to explore possibilities they might otherwise resist. Like Kristofferson's chains, structure can give us freedom.

Selling Change

I received the following email from a young couple who had completed the *Ranching For Profit School* two weeks earlier.

> We had a wonderful experience at the school but as I feared, my parents aren't as excited with the new ideas we brought home. They were very upset when we showed them the numbers and compared them to the RFP benchmarks. We proposed several alternatives but every idea only seems to anger and frustrate my folks. A few more years and I am sure that will change. Or is that what every younger generation rancher tells themself?

I wrote back that "regardless of how gently you may be offering your suggestions, your folks may be hearing, 'You've been screwing things up all of these years! We are going to fix it.' That would alienate anybody." Then I told them they needed to learn sales.

Sales? Absolutely. It is an essential skill in business and a skill most ranchers never learn. All of us are selling all the time. Whether it is a product, a point of view, an idea or a proposed change, it is all about sales.

Most people think that sales is about getting someone to buy something they don't need. It isn't. The real purpose of making a sale is to help someone solve their problem.

I made a sales call to this same couple when they first expressed interest in the school. My goal was not to pressure them to attend but to understand their problems and help them determine if the school had appropriate solutions. When I asked them if they remembered the call, they said, "Yes. Your 'sales' call is absolutely what sold us. You took the time and listened, and no, you weren't pushy, but we did need that phone call to nudge us to a yes."

That's sales. It is not an underhanded, sleazy, manipulative thing. It is a positive, mutually beneficial skill intended to produce win-win outcomes. The win for the customer is a problem solved. The win for the seller is compensation for the seller's time, energy, resources and the satisfaction of having helped the customer.

You don't sell change by talking about the change you want to make. You do it by exploring the cost of the problems you want to solve. The critical equation is:

$$\text{Value of the Solution} = \text{Cost of the Problem} - \text{Cost of the Solution}$$

If the value of the solution is greater than the cost of the problem minus the cost of the solution, you will make the sale. Recognize that the costs and values are not always measured in dollars and cents. The cost to us of the stress of a chronic problem may far outweigh the financial impact of that problem. Likewise, the value of ensuring that the ranch will support future generations is something more than just the income it will generate for those families.

Let's apply this to the young couple's situation. I suggested that they start by backing off the pressure: "Dad, sorry we came on strong about stuff from that school. We were pretty excited with some of the things we learned. We would like to go into that more with you sometime if you'd like to know more about it."

Then I suggested that they ask questions to understand the parent's issues and concerns and explore the cost of the problem: "How do you feel about the future of the ranch? My guess is that 10 or 20 years from now, you'd like this thing to be able to support you and Mom, us and eventually your grandchildren. To do all of that, isn't it going to have to make a bigger profit than it does today?" (Notice I didn't say that the ranch loses money today.) "Are you satisfied with our current profitability? How do you see this transition working? How do you think we can make it profitable enough to support us without relying on off-farm income? Do you even think it is possible?"

Sales is not about telling someone what they need and forcing them to buy. It is about helping them understand the full cost of the problem. Once you feel like you understand the problem and have explored its cost, explore potential solutions and their value.

They have to be hungry for a solution. And they need to be part of building the solution. Several years ago a doctor prescribed medication for me without consulting with me about it. I was supposed to take it four times a day. He didn't understand my schedule and it was really inconvenient to take the medication, so I didn't take it. As the problem persisted and grew worse, I met with him again. This time he listened as I described my schedule. He put me on a different dosage that I could take once each day. I took it and the problem was solved. The first time he did a lousy job of sales. The second time he did a good job. The solution must fit the problem *and* the people with the problem.

> What is life for if it isn't to help one another?

I start the sales training we do in *Executive Link* by asking, "How do you feel about sales?" Nearly everyone says they hate it. When I ask, "How do you feel when you are able to help people?" they often say that there is no better feeling. If that's the case, then we ought to love sales. It will be an essential skill for the young couple to learn if they want to change the course of the family ranch.

Separating the Land Business from the Livestock Business

A recent *Ranching For Profit School* graduate emailed me to ask for advice. He said he was having a hard time working through differences with his family on strategies and tactics required to turn their unprofitable business into a profitable one.

He'd shown that changing from a year-round March calving cow/calf operation to a seasonal custom grazing operation would be more profitable and free up capital, with which he suggested they pay down debt. Another option was to stay with cows but change the calving season to May and June, which would reduce, and in some years eliminate, the need for hay.

His folks weren't buying it. He said they resisted everything he suggested.

I offered some suggestions to help him get at their core concerns, and I have confidence they will resolve their issues and agree to a plan. However, when disagreements can't be settled between generations, it may be time to separate the land business from the operation of the enterprises. (It is often a good idea, even if there isn't a conflict.) This usually works something like this: Mom and Dad own the land and receive rent from whoever is using that land (probably the kids). The kids own or lease the assets used in the operating business. Depending on the scale of the operation, competitive rents and lease fees can be a comfortable living for the folks. If it isn't enough to provide a decent living, it may be that the scale wouldn't have been enough to support more than one family, even if the land and livestock were not separated.

> The land and the operating business should be seen as two separate entities, with the cattle, farming and other enterprises renting the land at the prevailing rate.

131

Separating the land business from the operation of enterprises is also a relatively simple way to get the next generation off to a flying and independent start without having the folks second-guess management decisions. They may second-guess the decisions anyway, but at least Junior has the authority to call the shots. And it will be Junior who will benefit from his smart decisions and take his lumps for the bad ones.

Brett Nix, a *Ranching For Profit School* alumnus from South Dakota, leases his parents' farm. He told me that separating the operating business from the land had been a difficult decision for everyone. One day, a few months after making the change, his mother told Brett about a conversation she'd just had with his father. His father told her, "Man, we should have done this a lot sooner."

Brett still involves his dad in decisions and appreciates his experience and insights. His dad has made helpful suggestions on the implementation of ideas that he had been against before they split the operating business from the land. Brett said, "I don't think he realized that he could still be part of things without carrying the burden that goes with making management decisions."

Separating the land from operations certainly simplifies things when there are off-farm stakeholders. They say that too many cooks spoil the stew. Well, too many cooks in operations is a recipe for chaos and conflict. It's hard to blame off-farm shareholders for wanting to have a say in management; after all, they often have millions of dollars tied up in the ranch and see little, if any, return.

It generally results in a stronger business and better relationships with shareholders if only one or two family members own the operating business. They rent the ranch, which in some cases may be owned by dozens of family members. Land expenses (e.g., property taxes) are deducted from the rents paid by operations. The balance is normally distributed to the shareholders, proportionate with their shares.

Even if the alumnus and his parents decide to continue in business together, as I suspect they will, they should still consider the land and the operations as two separate entities, with the cattle, farming and other enterprises paying market rate rent to the land business. This is the only way to see if the operating business is subsidizing the land business, if the land business subsidizes operations or if each is able to stand on its own. If the operating business can make a profit after paying fair market rent, you'll probably want to consider expanding the livestock operation by leasing someone else's place too.

Fool Me Once

Life isn't a fairy tale. Sometimes regardless of how good our idea is, how well we listen, how well we prepare and plan, we still run into a brick wall of resistance. Sometimes we don't all live happily ever after. I've had more than one *ProfitTips* reader write me to ask, "What now?"

The answer is simple, leave. Of course, leaving isn't simple and it sure isn't easy. But what's the alternative?

> Do the hard thing and life can be easy, but if you always do the easy thing, life will be hard.

If you are dissatisfied with the way things are, you only have three choices:

1. Change things.
2. Accept that you can't change things and leave.
3. Accept that you can't change things and learn to be happy with that.

The third option rarely works and usually makes everyone miserable for a long time.

The challenge is to know when to give up and move on.

Sometimes we are too quick to give up. I remember a young man attending a *Ranching For Profit School* I was teaching in Calgary, Alberta, whose frustration was palpable. That day he'd heard about separating the operating business from the land business. He knew that leasing the ranch from his parents could be his breakthrough, but he said with certainty, "There's no way Dad will agree to that!" Less than a year later he was leasing the ranch and his Dad was working part time as his hired hand.

Sometimes we wait and wait, hoping that it won't take an undertaker to facilitate change. One young couple I worked with recently said that they kept waiting for their folks to follow through on vague promises of handing over more responsibility and authority. After 10 years they were still waiting. They put the blame on the folks.

I asked, "When did you realize that your folks were unlikely to follow through?"

"Years ago," they said in unison.

I asked, "Knowing that your folks were not going to change, who made the decision to stay, you or your folks?"

It wasn't their folks making them unhappy. It was the couple's decision to stay. They looked at one another and realized that they could do something about their situation. A few months later they moved to manage a ranch in a neighboring state. They tell me the relationship with their folks has improved.

When you are working with rational people, it is usually possible to make changes that work in everyone's best interests. (If you are working with irrational people, all bets are off.) If the situation is intolerable and you've no hope of changing it, your best bet is to get out, and the sooner the better for everyone involved. The sooner you move on, the sooner you can get to work building your future and the sooner it removes the fly in the ointment for everyone else.

The Family in Family Business

- Business Is Business and Family Is Family

- You Don't Owe Your Kid a Job

- I'll Work for Free Because Someday Part of This Might Be Mine

- Waiting to Dance

- Nothing Sucks Like Succession

- Two Legacies

Business Is Business and Family Is Family

In a healthy family business there is a clear line separating business and family. In other words, business is business and family is family. But in most family businesses the line between work and family gets blurred. Am I talking to my parent or the CEO? My daughter or my employee? In ranching, where most of us live inside our businesses, the line may be non-existent. When we are at home we are at work, and when we are at work we are still at home.

This boundary between work and life is important. Without it, what we do becomes who we are. If what we do is who we are, who are we when we stop doing? How do we make the transition to the next generation? It often happens over Dad's dead body, literally. Without the line between work and life, how do we hold family members accountable in the business without having a food fight at the dinner table? (Or is it the boardroom?)

> The boundary between work and life is important. Without it, what we do becomes who we are. If what we do is who we are, who are we when we stop doing?

The line between family and business becomes sharper when we hold regular WOTB (Working *On* The Business) meetings. WOTB meetings focus on the important issues facing the business. They provide an effective forum for having business discussions and making strategic and tactical decisions.

We recommend that *Executive Link* members hold a WOTB meeting every month. They use these sessions to create their drought plan, establish employee policies for their ranch, develop their succession plan, make decisions on expansion, and tackle other issues important to the success of the business.

Executive Link members tell us that the results they get from holding regular WOTB meetings are powerful. They also tell us that actually holding the meetings is a hard habit to establish. On a family ranch it is easy to distract ourselves with WITB (Working *In* The Business).

Sometimes an *Executive Link* member will tell me with a little shame, "We need to hold more WOTB meetings." They are usually surprised when I ask, "Why?" After a moment's pause, they often say something like, "I thought you said we should." But the point isn't to hold a meeting. The point is to create a marketing plan, assess the potential of a new enterprise, devise a risk management strategy and do a dozen other things that every business needs to do. The WOTB meeting is just the vehicle through which we produce these results. By focusing on the results we need, our incentive to hold WOTB meetings goes up and our tendency to become distracted with WITB goes away.

It is probably unrealistic to keep business-related discussions out of the bedroom and away from the dinner table. If you are lying in bed staring at the ceiling in a cold sweat at 2 a.m. worrying about your cash flow, you need to be able to express those concerns. But that's WATB (Worrying About The Business) not WOTB. If you had held some effective WOTB meetings you'd probably be sleeping at 2 a.m.

You Don't Owe Your Kid a Job

Here's a test. Let's say you have a job opening for a ranch manager in your business. This is someone who will do everything from feeding cattle and fixing fences to projecting cash flow and making marketing decisions. There are two applicants for the job.

The first applicant grew up locally. He was in 4-H and FFA but never went to college. Instead he went to Australia where he worked as a jackaroo for three years. He then moved to Arizona where he worked for a fence contractor for a couple of years, after which he started his own fencing business. He had a small crew and made a modest profit. Ultimately his former employer purchased the business. He accepted a job managing a ranch for an absentee owner in Jackson Hole, Wyoming. There were a couple hundred cows. The ranch was primarily a retreat for the owner. It did not make a profit, but the owner was happy with the manager's performance.

The second applicant is another local kid. Also involved in 4-H and FFA, he went to college and received a degree in agricultural business. After receiving the degree, he went right back to the family farm, where he's spent the last 12 years putting up hay, feeding cows and mending fence.

The question is, which one would you hire?

The answer is, you would hire the one who is related to you. In other words, qualifications don't seem to count in family businesses as much as bloodlines, birth order and gender. When the candidate pool is limited to your gene pool, it makes for a pretty limited choice. That may work for the royal family, but if you want to make a profit, it's no way to pick an employee. If our kids are not the most qualified, hiring them may not be a smart move. Ranching is a tough business and success in the future will require quality management.

It's one thing for your kids to work in your business when they are young, but it's a different story when they are adults. We don't owe our adult children a living. Furthermore, bringing unqualified family members into the ranch isn't good for our kids, it isn't good for us, and it certainly isn't good for our business.

It isn't good for our kids because we set them up for failure. Most of our kids never acquire the skills needed to run a business. Knowing how to raise cattle isn't the same as knowing how to run a business that raises cattle. One reason the depression rate in agriculture is so high is that most ranchers never acquire the insights and skills needed to build and manage a profitable business.

It isn't good for us because, just when we bring Junior into the business (usually after high school or college), we've entered our own managerial prime. This can lead to conflict or resentment.

It isn't good for business either. I recently saw data showing that over 20% of heirs fail to keep the ranches they inherit because they lack the management skills needed to run a profitable business.

When we do bring our kids into the business, we tend to do it the wrong way. We usually put them to work doing the things that they are good at. Unfortunately, those usually aren't the things that need to be done. We've got it backwards. We should start with what needs to be done.

What needs to be done? Every business has three primary needs: production, marketing and finance. Most of us focus on production to the exclusion of marketing and finance. If their skills match the need we have (usually marketing or finance), we might be smart to hire them. If they don't match, we should either make sure they get the training they'll need to be successful or hire someone else.

Many of our *Executive Link* members who have tackled succession issues started by establishing a policy and procedure for bringing family members into their businesses. They work with their kids to identify the skills their business needs in production, sales, finance and human resources in order to be successful. They build a career development plan, mapping a path for developing these skills. It often includes working for someone else for five to 10 years to gain knowledge and experience. This way they bring more experience back to the ranch and can make more of a contribution to the success of the business. In some cases, rather than carving out room for the kids, the kids are expected to launch a new income-generating enterprise themselves. This is a surefire way to test their entrepreneurial talent.

Please understand, I am all for keeping the ranch in the family, but wouldn't it be better if our kids are people we would hire even if they weren't related to us? We owe it to ourselves, our kids and our businesses to make sure that if we bring our kids into the business, we do it the right way.

> Employing unqualified family members in the family business isn't good for them, it isn't good for you, it isn't good for the family and it certainly isn't good for the business.

I'll Work for Free Because Someday Some of This Might Be Mine

I received an email from an alumnus who had been talking to a young rancher about the work that he and his brother did and the salary they were paid. The brothers, both in their 20's, were sons of the owner. They paid themselves a fraction of what they would have had to pay someone else to do their work. They reasoned that it would be wrong to take a full salary because they stood to "inherit a portion of the ranch someday."

Inheritance should have nothing to do with it. Employment and ownership are two entirely different things. Problems start when we mix the two up, especially if there are off-farm people who have a stake in the ranch. By working for less than their work is worth, the brothers may start to feel as though Mom and Dad *owe* them. The implied promise that "someday this will all (or some portion of this will) be yours" is dangerous as well. Folks don't *owe* their kids an inheritance. Mom and Dad may change their mind.

If the brothers get a bigger slice of the pie when Mom and Dad pass away than other siblings who don't live on the ranch, those siblings may not take kindly to the boys getting "special treatment." After all, even though the boys didn't get paid a lot, the ranch provided them with a lot of perks, not the least of which is living in what the off-farm kids remember as "paradise" when they grew up.

> Employment in and ownership of a business are two entirely different things. Problems start when we mix the two.

These brothers aren't alone. Many young people coming back to the farm take a low wage thinking they will build "sweat equity" in the business. Hardly any of them ever quantify the value of their sweat and most of them have a highly inflated idea of the equity that their sweat is worth. Let's say you come back to the family farm and take a wage that is $10,000 less than we would have to pay a non-family member to do the same work ($10,000 of sweat equity). If our ranch is valued at $10 million, your sweat equity translates to a 1/1,000th share in the ranch each year. At that rate, you'll have gained a 5% stake in 50 years, assuming the ranch doesn't appreciate in value.

Keep it clean. Pay Junior the salary you'd have to pay a non-family employee to do the job. If he wants to start building equity in the business, he can buy shares with whatever salary is left after his living expenses, provided the owners are of a mind to sell. If the business can't afford to pay the wage, tough. You couldn't refuse to pay non-family labor just because the business can't afford it. You'd have to find a way to do it. In the case of family, they can trade the salary they are owed for equity or offer to loan the money back to the business. If they loan it back, the loan and the interest it accrues must be documented.

The wage should be fair and the value of fringe benefits and perks (business-supplied housing, vehicle, insurance, beef, etc.) should be documented so everyone, including off-farm shareholders, knows exactly what's going on.

If the brothers actually do own some or all of the ranch one day, they'll find that as important as "Who owns what?" is "Who runs what?" Too often sons and daughters are lured back to the ranch with the expectation of taking on meaningful responsibility, only to spend a decade or more as a hired hand. An organization chart showing the basic roles in the business is a useful tool to make current and future roles and responsibilities clear to everyone.

You might think, "An organization chart for a family ranch? Isn't that overkill? After all, we aren't IBM." But you and IBM both have the same needs. IBM has to produce a product and watch its costs. So do you. IBM has to market its product in a competitive marketplace where buyers have lots of buying options. So do you. IBM has to manage its money. You have capital availability and cash flow issues too. Administration, taxes, government regulations? Both you and Big Blue have to deal with all of them. People problems? You both have them. There is one big difference between you and IBM. IBM has a whole department to deal with those issues. You don't; and if some of your employees are family members, your people issues are actually more complex and more important than IBM's.

Function	IBM	You
Production	✓	✓
Sales	✓	✓
Finance	✓	✓
Administration	✓	✓
Human Resources	✓	?

The biggest difference between most family businesses and IBM is the scale. IBM has so many employees that people are able to specialize in one area. With fewer people, we have to wear more hats, but the number of hats is size neutral.

Whether it's you or IBM, all businesses share the same basic functions. Your organization chart (on the next page) shows who is currently responsible for each of these functions. While several people may make contributions in each of these areas, only one person can be accountable for the results. By showing who that person is you will avoid misunderstandings about roles and responsibilities.

Your management succession plan projects your organization chart into the future so that it is clear to everyone who will be responsible for what, when. You can then map out a career

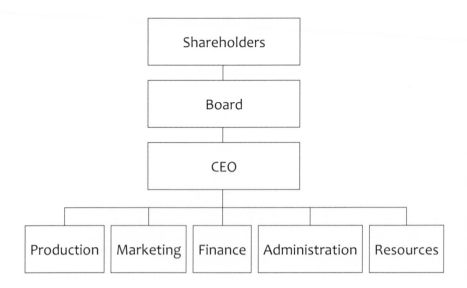

development plan for each position to make sure each person has the skills needed to be successful in that role.

Being able to say, "In five years you'll be in charge of marketing and here's the training you'll need to be successful," is a lot more meaningful than saying, "Ready or not, someday this will all be yours."

Waiting to Dance

At the *Ranching For Profit School* we teach a four-step strategic planning process to help business owners create a shared vision for their ranch and a plan to achieve it. It starts with the very simple question, "Looking into the future five or 10 years, what do you want?" When we say *you*, we mean *you*. Many of us try to answer the question by thinking about what everyone else wants. But the question isn't, "What do *you* think your spouse, your parents, your siblings or your children want?" The question is, "What do *you* want?" By drawing out of each person what he or she wants and discussing the underlying needs, we create a picture of what the collective you, the stakeholders in the business, want. It is a very powerful process.

Mom and Dad often struggle with this process. They haven't really thought about what they want for a long time. They have spent the last 20 years thinking about what the kids want and, depending on their situation, what their aging parents need. Thinking of themselves first doesn't come naturally. Sometimes they even feel a little guilty about it.

I've seen it a hundred times. The kids are 22 and 17. Mom and Dad are 50ish and aren't sure what the kids really want. The kids don't know themselves. At that age, most of us didn't either. It was a time in most of our lives when we discovered the world *out there* and discovered ourselves, testing our boundaries and learning what we were capable of.

Mom and Dad would like the kids to be part of the ranch someday, if that's what the kids decide they want. But the kids aren't ready to decide. So Mom and Dad wait. Creating a vision and planning are put on hold. Without a vision to inspire them and a plan to guide them, they

> If you create a business that you are passionate about, it will become a magnet for the next generation.

drift. Ironically, what they are doing (or aren't doing) in hopes that the kids will want to come back makes it less likely that the kids will want to, or be able to, come back.

When I meet people who are waiting for their kids to decide, I picture a high school dance. I imagine a boy who'd like to dance with a pretty girl but is too shy to ask. He sits waiting and hoping that she will walk across the room and ask him. Fat chance. The longer he sits there, the less likely it becomes. If he were to just start dancing with someone, she might be more inclined to say "yes." Seeing that he knows how to cut a rug and have fun makes him an even more attractive partner. Even if she says "no," he still got to dance.

There's nothing more debilitating than indecision. Sitting on the sidelines while the world around us changes, without establishing a goal or enacting a plan, is like waiting for that girl to ask you to dance. If you create a business that you are passionate about, it will become a magnet for the next generation. They may even ask if they can join the dance.

Nothing Sucks Like Succession

You know how difficult it was to have *that* talk with your kids about the facts of life? There is a talk that you need to have with your family that is even more difficult. It's about the facts of death.

We make all sorts of excuses to avoid it. In the short term, avoiding the discussion seems less stressful than dealing with what may be difficult and delicate issues. We know that the long-term consequences of avoiding it can be disastrous. In the short term, the price of avoidance is ongoing stress and guilt.

Nobody wants to talk about it. Dad and Mom don't want to talk about it because it means facing their mortality. Furthermore, they see the ranch as their legacy and want all of the kids to share in that, but they know the ranch can't support everyone. They love all of their kids and want to treat them fairly, but somehow the equal distribution of assets doesn't seem "fair." Then there's the gold digger that Junior married and that *bum* your baby girl calls her husband. Yes, they've been married for 10 years, but you know it isn't going to last.

The kids don't want to bring it up either. They don't want to be seen as ungrateful vultures waiting for the folks to die so they can pick at the remains. But the clock is ticking and they need to know what the future holds. The more years they invest on the ranch the less employable they become elsewhere.

No wonder we don't want to deal with this. Unfortunately, if we don't we will have placed a huge burden on the people we love after we die, and that's the *best*-case scenario. More likely we will have sown seeds of resentment that will germinate under the unbelievable stress we will have put on them and on their relationships with one another. Oh, and while all of that is happening, our primary heir will be our Uncle Sam.

Ultimately most business owners need professional advisors to determine the best vehicles to accomplish their goals. But before we meet with them, there are some things we can do to lay a foundation for using them efficiently and creating the best plan possible. Here are some tips:

Succession doesn't start when you die

You have worked your entire life doing, doing, doing. It is not reasonable to expect to stop on a dime. Stan Parsons once told me, "You can't retire *from* ranching. You have to retire *to* something." Whatever it is you retire to doesn't just appear. It's something you have to create well before you retire.

It may be that after control, and perhaps even ownership, of the operating business passes to another generation, you are still very involved in the operation. It is important to think about the level of involvement and control you will want. How much flexibility do you want? How much income will you need?

One solution mentioned earlier in this section and enacted by many ranch families is to separate the operating business from the land business. Mom and Dad own the land and rent it to one or more of the kids who own the operating business. That business may lease the livestock and equipment or replace them with its own. Either way, the kids call the shots in that business, often using Mom and Dad as a senior advisor and a hired hand. Mom and Dad collect the rent as their retirement income.

> "Companies don't suddenly decide to have a transition any more than a woman suddenly decides to give birth."
>
> Don Jonovic

Define owner value

The ranch shouldn't just be an asset to pass on when you die. It ought to be a thriving business providing value for all of the stakeholders before *and* after that fateful day. Delivering what we call *owner value* begins with defining it. The formula is simple:

$$\text{Owner Value} = \text{Investment} + \text{Return}$$

Our investment includes the money, time, energy, emotion and sacrifices we've made for the business. Foregoing college or another career to come back to the ranch because you were needed constitutes a large investment.

The return may involve more than money, as well. For some people the return can be negative. Just ask a ranch wife I met who tolerates barbs from her mother-in-law on a daily basis about negative returns.

It is important to get specific on these issues. For example, we might all agree that profit is important, but we may not agree on what we ought to do with the profit. Should we put it in an off-farm investment, put it back in the business, use it to build reserves or distribute it as dividends to shareholders? We need to reach a consensus.

Once owner value is defined, targets should be established and a plan created to achieve those targets.

Who, what, and how

In *The Ultimate Legacy*, Dr. Don Jonovic says that the most critical issues in an estate plan are:

1. Who will run what?
2. Who will own what?
3. How will you make sure you have the capacity to pay the taxes so that the first two things can actually happen?

The transfer of authority can be even more contentious than the transfer of assets. Assets are just things and things can be replaced. With authority comes control, and when it is given it implies respect.

Many families confuse ownership with management. Just because someone owns a business doesn't mean they ought to be running it. Birth order and gender should not have any influence over roles in the family business. Some families would be smart to hire professional non-family management to run the business. Regardless of who manages what, management positions should be based on competency.

The basis of a management succession plan is a projected organization chart showing who will be in what roles at some point in the future. Accompanying the chart should be a career development plan showing the experience and training each person needs to be successful in the role.

Asset transfer is another potentially divisive issue. Intellectually we know that the equal distribution of assets isn't necessarily fair. Yet emotionally we may have a hard time justifying the unequal distribution. The problem is compounded when all of our assets are tied up in the ranch. That makes it very difficult to distribute assets equally without wrecking the operation.

One solution may be to leave the land in an undivided interest to our children. There should be some kind of buy-sell agreement in place so if one sibling wants to take his money and run, he can do so without breaking up the ranch. Typically the purchase value of the shares would be steeply discounted from the market value of the property. This way it doesn't force the others to sell out to satisfy the one who wants out. The operating business would be given, sold or leased to just one heir. That heir would pay market rate rent to the land ownership group of which he or she is a part.

Pay the damn taxes

No one wants to pay more taxes than necessary, but don't let tax avoidance drive your plan. Look for ways to minimize your tax liability *after* you have decided how to grow and protect owner value, provide for your needs in retirement, transition the management to the next generation and distribute the assets of your estate.

Placing tax avoidance as your number one priority can be a very expensive strategy. One family I know jumped at an opportunity to avoid a potentially big tax bill without doing these other things first. It set the stage for a long, expensive and emotional legal nightmare for everyone.

Most family ranches don't make it to a third generation, and most of those that make it to a third don't make it to a fourth. Discussing these issues with your family can save everyone time and money and lead to a better plan.

There is life after death, or at least there can be. If you want your family to have a life on the ranch after you meet your maker, you need to talk to them about the facts of death.

Two Legacies

Legacy is a powerful concept. Perhaps that is because we see our legacy as a form of immortality. In some families it has survived generations now long gone. Many people I work with feel a deep obligation to carry on the family's legacy. A family's legacy can be rich with meaning and a powerful source of inspiration. Unfortunately, the power of a legacy is often more destructive than constructive.

I was surprised when I looked up legacy to see Webster define it as "money or property left to someone in a will." I have never thought of a legacy as simply *things*. If that's all it is, it wouldn't be nearly as powerful a concept. Webster misses the point. A legacy is the meaning represented by those things. In fact, a legacy doesn't have to be passed on through things at all.

In my mom's final years and just after her passing, I feel like my sister and I grew closer. My sister and I didn't fight over our mother's modest estate. We each expressed concern for the other's interests and wanted to make sure the other's needs were met. My mother's legacy wasn't in the form of physical assets. It was in the values she instilled in my sister and me.

I've met with many multi-generational farm and ranch families working through succession issues. Some are poised to go on for many more generations. Others have reached the end of the road. There are a lot of things that go into making a multi-generational family business thrive from one generation to the next, but the meaning and form of their legacy is as important as any of them. Those families for whom the legacy they inherit and perpetuate is more about *values* than *things* tend to endure and prosper. Those for whom the legacy is more about things than values won't last.

For a lot of farm and ranch families, the legacy seems to center on a particular piece of property. When there are three generations buried in the family plot on the hill beside your home, it is easy to see your legacy as a place, a herd of cattle or some other "thing."

If your business was in town, it would be different. If Smith and Son's Manufacturing sold the obsolete factory that your great-grandfather built and moved to a modern facility they leased on the other side of town, it would be emotional but it wouldn't carry the same drama as selling the family ranch. Of course, there aren't three generations of Smiths buried under the parking lot.

I recently spoke to one man with a young family who was determined to "carry on the family legacy." For him that meant staying on the family ranch. But the capacity of the ranch was only 150 cows. That may have been enough in Granddad's day, but it isn't enough now. Town had moved closer, and the neighbors had sold out to developers who divided their places into ranchettes. Land values were astronomical. To rent anything of any size meant driving a good hour, one way. In addition to working on the ranch, both he and his wife had jobs in town. They told me that they would give anything to quit their jobs and ranch full time, but they weren't going to be the ones to end the "legacy."

> You can honor someone's legacy without sacrificing your life and happiness to follow it.

If they were to sell and move they could buy a place a few hundred miles away, with four or five times the capacity, that wouldn't need to be subsidized with off-farm income. I wonder how his parents and grandparents, now gone, would feel if they could see how hard their heirs work and how much they sacrifice to keep the place. Perhaps they'd consider themselves failures for not infusing enough pioneer spirit in their heirs to do what they need to do to build a thriving business and a happy life. Perhaps a more pertinent question is, "What kind of legacy are we passing on to our children?" Is our intention to pass on the burden of maintaining the family place, regardless of the personal and financial cost? Perhaps we'd rather push this decision off on our children when they inherit the place.

I often suggest to people struggling with this issue that every family has two legacies. The first is the legacy of the pioneer. The pioneer left home and blazed a trail to establish the ranch. The second legacy comes from the builder. The builder added to what the pioneer started. The point is that we all have a choice as to which legacy we are going to follow, the pioneer or the builder. Either path you choose honors one of your family's legacies. You can honor a legacy without sacrificing your life and happiness to follow it.

3. Profitable Businesses

It Isn't Sustainable
If It Isn't Profitable

The healthiest land I see and the happiest families I meet are almost always part of the most profitable businesses. Profit is a quality of life issue. *Ranching For Profit School* alumnus Derek Schwanebeck put it this way: "When we focused on our life, all we did was work our butts off and get frustrated. When we focused on profit, our life got so much better."

Aspiring to Have Tax Problems

- What's Wrong with Profit?

- Aspiring to Have Tax Problems

- What Is Your Profit For?

- Understanding Profit

What's Wrong with Profit?

These days it seems like profit is a dirty word. Perhaps it is Wall Street's obsession with the single bottom line: return on investment. In the movie *Wall Street*, Michael Douglas' line, "Greed is good" is the epitome of the single bottom line mentality.

Greed is bad. But sustainable profit isn't about greed. Sustainable profit has multiple bottom lines: economic, ecological, personal and societal. A business isn't sustainable if it doesn't make an economic profit, but it must make that profit without degrading the resources it uses or exploiting the people who produce it. And it must do all of this without externalizing costs to the public.

I can understand the public's misgivings about profit. Too often companies are focused only on next quarter's returns. They are accountable to shareholders who have no investment in and no accountability to local communities. Too often they use exploitive practices that mine biological capital. The products they produce appear to be inexpensive, but they come with a very hefty price tag once we consider all the externalized costs. In agriculture those externalized costs include degraded environmental quality (e.g., the dead zone in the Gulf of Mexico), less flavorful food (e.g., have you eaten a store-bought tomato recently?) and higher taxes.

Of course, there are a lot of farmers and ranchers who are building organic matter, protecting watersheds, and improving wildlife habitat. They provide lots of valuable services and benefits to the public while producing wholesome, nutritious food. We don't tell that story very effectively. And it takes only a visible minority who abuse their land and animals to give us all a black eye.

It isn't just the public that turns negative when we talk about profit. Some farmers and ranchers get defensive too. As soon as I bring up the idea of ranching for profit, I see some ranchers fold their arms and roll their eyes.

We have been told for so long, in so many ways, by so many people that ranching isn't profitable that deep down many ranchers now believe it. The old joke about what a rancher would do if he won the lottery—keep ranching until it's all gone—speaks volumes. If someone starts talking about increasing profit, it is natural for them to view the heretic with a hefty dose of skepticism. Many people seem more comfortable with *Ranching For Less Loss* than they are with *Ranching For Profit*.

I worked with a rancher to develop a grazing cell to improve the health and productivity of the land. When I told his father-in-law, who owned the property, what we were doing, why we were doing it and the results I expected to see, he said, "I'll *believe* it when I *see* it."

Next year, the results were better than I had expected. Among other things, carrying capacity had increased by 50% and the dominant weed had been replaced with grass. Walking over the range with the father-in-law, I challenged him, saying, "You said you'd believe it when you see it." He responded, "I'll *see* it when I *believe* it." I think he really did see the physical changes on the land, but his paradigm about the management of cattle and land was so strong that he couldn't acknowledge the value of the dramatic changes. Instead, he explained at length why the changes we'd made were a bad idea.

I think that many ranchers have lived so long with the *ranching is not profitable* paradigm that even when they encounter a situation that is profitable, or opportunities that could make their businesses profitable, they just can't see it. Seeing is believing, but sometimes you have to believe it to see it.

> Seeing is believing, but sometimes you have to believe it to see it.

The unprofitability paradigm is powerful and highly contagious. Steer clear of those who suffer from it (and they do suffer) and connect yourself with positive, forward-thinking ranchers.

Aspiring to Have Tax Problems

Over the years I've met many bankers who know finance inside and out, but they often don't have a very good handle on economics. What's the difference?

In economics, we ask two questions:

1. Is it profitable?
2. How do I make it more profitable?

In finance, we ask two very different questions:

1. Can I afford to do it? (Where will I find the startup capital I need?)
2. Once I get started, how will the cash flow?

There's actually a third issue when it comes to money: taxes. A lot of people prioritize these three issues exactly backwards. They make their top priority avoiding taxes. Finance becomes secondary and economics is only an afterthought.

In an effort to avoid taxes, a lot of people make some pretty bad economic decisions. There are hundreds of thousands of monuments on farms and ranches erected in the name of tax avoidance. These monuments include fixed assets like expensive buildings, new machinery, overpriced registered livestock, etc. By buying them before the year ends, we can reduce our tax liability. That these things never return a penny is bad enough, but even worse is that they cost a pretty penny to maintain. This makes it much more difficult to make a profit in the future.

I tell people at *The Ranching For Profit School* that economics *always* precedes finance and that they should aspire to have income tax problems! Too bad, you made a lot of money! Sure, you'll want to minimize taxes, but not at the expense of reducing your profitability. It doesn't do any good to worry about hanging on to your money if you don't make any money to hang on to.

It may be smart to pre-pay operating expenses that you'll incur in the coming year in order to reduce your tax bite now. But it is just plain stupid to buy things that you don't really need. Our short-term focus on avoiding taxes today can make it much more difficult to make a profit tomorrow.

Economics always comes before finance

Let's say I found a great investment. If I invest $100,000, by the end of the year it will grow to $200,000. That's a 100% return! Economically, this is a great deal. The question we have to ask now is, "How will I come up with $100,000?" That's a financial question. I will also need to figure out when I'll get my income. How will the cash flow? If it all comes at the end of the year I'll have to figure out how to pay my bills in the meantime. Those are all financial questions.

What if I found an alternative investment opportunity? This one also required a $100,000 investment but is guaranteed to lose $50,000! Economically, that's a horrible deal. Since I don't want to lose $50,000, do I need to bother with figuring out how to finance it? Of course not! That's why we *always* start with economics before turning to finance.

Only after considering the economics and finances do we look at the tax consequences and explore strategies to minimize our taxes without sacrificing profitability.

Think about it this way: economics is the engine that drives your business and finance is the gas that starts it up and makes it go (cash flow).

We start down the road to sustainability by tuning up our economic engine *before* tackling the financial questions. It doesn't do much good to pour more gasoline into an engine that won't run.

> Economics: Do we want to do it? Finance: Can we afford to do it?

What Is Your Profit For?

A *Ranching For Profit School* alumnus was talking to me about his financial goals. I asked how much profit he wanted to make. He told me he figured he needed $20,000 to live. I reminded him that his salary or draw must be deducted as an overhead cost before calculating profit. I asked again how much profit he wanted. It was clear he didn't have a target when he said, "I guess $10,000 would be good."

I asked what he would do with a $10,000 profit. He said he'd never had any reserves and he'd use it to start a savings program.

> Money is only important when put in the context of what it will be used for.

"So your profit is for building financial security," I said.

I pushed a little further, asking what he'd do if he made a $50,000 profit. He said that he'd pay down his debt. "So your profit is for building financial security and getting the debt under control," I said.

Then I asked, "What would you do if you had a $75,000 profit?" In an instant he said that he'd go on a golf vacation. "So your profit is for building financial security, getting debt under control and rewarding yourself," I added.

Finally I asked, "What would you do with the money if your business made a $100,000 profit?" Without blinking an eye he named an organization to which he said he'd like to make a big donation. "So your profit is for building financial security, controlling the debt, rewarding yourself and supporting causes you believe in."

After a pause I asked him again how much profit he wanted to make. He was no longer satisfied with a $10,000 target and he named a much higher amount.

Very few people are motivated by money. For most of us money is only important when put in the context of what it will be used for. Monetary targets are important, but having a clear picture of how the money will be used when those targets are achieved will be much more motivating.

Understanding Profit

Stan Parsons used to say conventional ranching is financially unattractive and economically unrewarding. Most ranches earn a very low return on investment, have inadequate cash flow and operate at an economic loss.

If that's the case, why don't ranchers go broke? It is simple: they subsidize their ranches with off-farm income, inherited wealth and working for free. How many ranchers would be ranching today if they hadn't inherited their ranches?

There are only three choices in any business:
1. We can go out of business (bankruptcy).
2. We can subsidize the business.
3. We can make it profitable.

If we want to make a profit, we need to start by understanding what profit is.

Ask most people and they'll tell you profit is income minus expenses. But profit looks at more than just cash in and out. Profit is the total *value* produced minus the total cost of producing that value. The value produced and the costs of production often include things other than cash.

On the value side, consider someone who retains their calves as replacement heifers or stockers. Those calves may not have produced cash income this year, but they did add value to the business. That needs to be accounted for. Rather than focus on income, we calculate *gross* product. Gross product measures the total value produced, whether it was realized in the form of cash or a change in inventory value.

Just as there are forms of non-cash income, we also need to account for non-cash costs. Consider a dead cow. When she dies, cash doesn't leave the business, but the value of our inventory goes down. That's a cost. Other non-cash costs include depreciation on facilities or equipment and unpaid labor.

Just as some costs are not cash expenses, some cash expenses are not costs. For example, when I buy a replacement for the cow that died, I may pay for it with cash, but in return I get an animal equal to the value of the cash I paid. The purchase was a cash expense because money left my business. It was not an economic cost because my business did not lose value. I simply changed the form in which I held the asset.

At *The Ranching For Profit School* we us a pragmatic definition for profit. We ask, can you:

- Pay rent for all of the land you use (even the land you own),
- Pay the full cost of labor (even yourself),
- Pay interest on all of the assets you use as though everything, including your animals, were financed by a bank, and
- Pay all of your other production costs and make a positive return on your investment?

If you can, you are making a profit. If you can't, like most other ranchers, you are making an economic loss.

Why include the cost of rent if you own the land? There are several important reasons. The land business is different from the livestock business. Charging rent to the livestock business is the only way to tell if the land business is subsidizing the livestock business, or if the livestock business is subsidizing the land business. More importantly, if your livestock business makes a profit paying the going rate for pasture rent to your land business, it tells you that growing your business by renting additional pasture is probably a good idea.

Most ranchers subsidize their operations by working for less than it would cost to replace themselves. To determine your real profit you must include what it would cost to replace the work you do, whether you take a draw on the ranch or not.

Including unpaid labor or, even better, actually paying the labor you use (including yourself) is important for several reasons. Let's compare the profitability of two ranches. One earns a $40,000 profit, the other makes a $10,000 loss. The first business consists of a couple who works 70 hours a week on the farm. They take a draw of about $20,000 each year. They get by on the income and health insurance provided by a full-time job one of them has in town.

The ranch showing a $10,000 loss on the books takes the same amount of labor but pays a wage of $70,000 to the couple and pays for health insurance. Do you really think that the first business is $50,000 more profitable than the second? When you factor in the difference in salaries and the cost of health insurance, it is at least $50,000 less profitable!

Be realistic with the salary. I asked a bank vice president who was retiring to a ranch he bought, "How much do you plan to pay yourself?"

"I want to replace my bank salary," he said.

When I asked what work he intended to perform to earn it he said, "I love to irrigate." That's not going to cut it. If you are going to irrigate, you should pay yourself irrigator wages. If you plan to be an effective CEO, then CEO wages are called for.

Most of us wear many hats in the business. If we wear a cowboy hat 80% of the time and a manager's hat 20% of the time, our wage should be 80% cowboy and 20% manager. In *Executive Link*, if someone has not included the draw for family members working on the ranch, we write in $45,000 for the first person and $35,000 for each additional person.

Imagine you want to start a ranch from scratch. You don't have deep pockets and can't subsidize it and you can't rely on off-farm income. You'd have to rent the land, pay the labor, pay interest on the money you borrowed to buy livestock and equipment, and cover all of the production costs that established ranchers would face. You'd have to make a positive return to stay in business. If you can do that, you are ranching for profit.

> The *Ranching For Profit* Definition for Profit
> ✓ Pay rent for the land
> ✓ Pay the full cost for labor
> ✓ Pay interest on all assets (including your livestock)
> ✓ Pay all other production costs
> And make a positive return on your investment.

Ranching for Profit

- The Three Secrets for Increasing Profit

- Management in a Bottle

- Growth Is Not a Strategy

- One Size Doesn't Fit All

- Three Questions for Diversification

- The Rule of Holes

The Three Secrets for Increasing Profit

There are only three ways to increase profit. At Ranch Management Consultants we call them *the three secrets*. They are:
1. Reduce overhead costs
2. Improve gross margin per unit
3. Increase turnover

Reducing overhead costs

Overhead costs are those costs that don't change much as livestock numbers change. Most overheads fall into one of two categories: land or labor. Any costs related to land (e.g., repairs to fences, corrals, pipelines, water troughs, leases) are land overheads. Likewise, any costs related to labor (e.g., salaries and benefits, vehicles and equipment costs) are labor overheads. Economists sometimes call these fixed costs. But they are not fixed; they can be changed, and that is one of the three secrets for increasing profit.

Improve gross margin per unit

Gross margin is a measure of the economic efficiency of your livestock. It is calculated by subtracting the *direct costs* of production from *gross product:*

Gross Product – Direct Costs = Gross Margin

Direct costs are those costs that increase or decrease as cow numbers increase or decrease. Direct costs include feed, health, freight, marketing commissions, and interest on livestock loans. Gross product refers to the gross value of production. This includes livestock sales minus purchases. It also includes changes in the value of your herd. We divide the total gross margin by the number of animals in the herd to calculate gross margin per unit. Increasing gross margin per unit (the efficiency of production) is the second of the three secrets for increasing profit.

We calculate profit by subtracting overhead costs from the total gross margin:

Gross Margin – Overhead Costs = Profit

Increase turnover

Turnover refers to the total volume produced by an enterprise. It consists of the number of units in an enterprise and the number of enterprises. If gross margin is positive, increasing turnover will increase profit as long as it doesn't increase land or labor costs or damage the resource base.

Historically, as an industry we have tried to increase profit by increasing production (increasing gross product). This strategy has made us more productive but has not made us more profitable. In fact, we have become more reliant than ever on off-farm income.

Part of the problem is fairly obvious: the increased production has resulted from, among other things, increasing direct costs (e.g., feed, health products). But there is more to the story. Those direct costs had to be administered by someone (increasing labor overheads), somewhere (increasing land overheads). On most conventionally run ranches, overhead costs account for 60 to 80% of total costs. These ranches are often very productive. Ironically, the cost of building and maintaining the infrastructure they use to support that production usually makes them unprofitable.

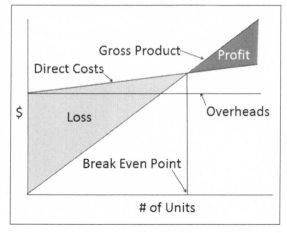

Imagine a chain with three economic links: overheads, gross margin per unit, and turnover. If the gross margin link is weak, strengthening the overhead and turnover links won't make the chain stronger. In fact, they may make the chain weaker by putting more stress on the weak link.

The four keys or the three secrets?

An article in a well-known industry publication recently caught my eye. The headline read, *The Big Four Management Strategies for Today's Rancher*. According to the article, the four key factors determining profit are: controlling feed costs, managing reproduction, planned marketing, and optimizing performance. These are important considerations, but they aren't the four most important things affecting profit.

The four keys in the magazine article all focus on improving gross margin, but none will help reduce overhead costs or do anything to increase turnover. Since overhead costs account for most of the costs on most ranches, and most ranches work well below economies of scale for the labor and equipment they have, reducing overheads and increasing turnover are at least as important as improving gross margin.

Our focus as an industry used to be on the weaning weight of the calf. The enlightened experts now tell us to focus on the weight weaned per cow using their four keys, but they completely ignore overhead costs and turnover. Trying to make a profit by focusing on the "four keys" is like playing cards with two-thirds of the deck missing. The three secrets trump the four keys.

• • •

There were several interesting comments on our blog in response to my contention that there is no such thing as a "fixed" cost. My point was that the term "fixed" implies that these costs can't be changed, and since costs that most economists would call "fixed" account for 60 to 80% of the costs on most ranches, we need to challenge this assumption. In fact, many of our alumni have dramatically reduced these costs, proving that they don't have to be "fixed."

One agricultural economist suggested that I "seek the services of a qualified production economist/business management specialist to review, rephrase and republish this article, as there are a number of technical issues that you have misrepresented." He went on to say that my approach was shortsighted and he encouraged people to subsidize one enterprise with another (I think our alumni would vigorously disagree). He offered his services to set me straight.

Another response to the article came from an Australian alumnus of *The Ranching For Profit School*. He wrote, "That was close to the best bit of advice I've ever read."

Our approach to assessing the economic and financial health of businesses is unconventional. It isn't intended for accountants, the IRS or academics. It's for people who want to make a sustainable profit from farming and ranching. We don't consider any costs fixed and we don't allocate overheads back to enterprises. AND our clients don't need a team of government economists to interpret their numbers for them. Most importantly, it helps them increase their sustainable profit.

> **The Three Secrets for Increasing Profit:**
> 1. Reduce overhead costs
> 2. Improve the gross margin per unit
> 3. Increase turnover

Look in any farming or ranching publication and you'll find articles about cutting your feed costs, increasing the efficiency of your health program or trimming variable costs like herbicide and fertilizer. But you won't find anyone who challenges land, labor and other overhead costs. That's because everyone believes they are fixed. By challenging these costs, thousands of our clients around the world have radically reduced their costs and proved that overheads don't have to be "fixed." That's an essential paradigm shift if you want to ranch for profit.

Management in a Bottle

I receive several mainstream livestock magazines every month. I scan the contents, occasionally mark an article to read later and sometimes I actually will come back and read it. Often what really catches my eye are the ads. Next time you pick up one of these publications, look at the ads. Ask yourself two questions:

1. What are they trying to sell me?
2. What is the true cost of this product?

Let's take a look at the ads in a recent issue of a popular beef industry magazine. On the inside cover is a full-page ad with a picture of a chain with a padlock and the caption, *To protect your cows. To protect your calves. To protect your future.* It is advertising a BVD vaccine. What are they trying to sell? Improved herd health, which should increase cow productivity. The economic term for the value of production is gross product. In essence, the ad encourages us to increase gross product. Of course, the vaccine isn't free. The more cows we have, the more vaccine we need. The vaccine is a direct cost.

The headline of the next ad, another full-pager, is, *For better fly control, get with the program.* It is advertising insecticide-laced ear tags. Using this product could improve animal performance. Like the previous ad, it is encouraging us to increase gross product. Like the vaccine, the ear tags aren't free. As herd size goes up, so will the number of ear tags we'll need. The ear tags are a direct cost.

The next full page ad says I will get an *extra 17 pounds of weight gain per head* if I use a certain feed additive that I can't even pronounce, let alone spell. What are they selling? Increased weight gain equals increased production per animal equals increased gross product. Like the ear tags, the feed additive is a direct cost.

More than 60% of the space in this magazine is advertising. About two-thirds of the ads are selling products intended to increase gross product, and all of these inputs are direct costs to us. There is no doubt that many of the inputs advertised will, under the right conditions, increase gross product. The gross product generated may even exceed the direct cost of the input. But the direct costs are not the only costs. These direct costs don't reflect the land and labor overheads that are required to give the shot, feed the feed, or provide the support required to realize the "improvements." And while these products may increase production per animal, they don't do anything to help us carry more animals. The real question is, "Will increasing gross product increase profit?" The answer is often "No." Even when the answer is "Yes," there are often other actions that will produce a much bigger profit.

My favorite ad is a two-page spread that shows a green pasture with cows grazing in the foreground, and in the background the green pasture is being poured out of a giant bottle. The headline reads, *Pasture management doesn't get any easier than this.*

Next time you pick up one of the livestock industry magazines, take a look at the ads and think about what they are selling and the true costs of using the products. Ask yourself how often they use code words like "efficiency" that really mean gross product. Have these products really made us more efficient or just more productive? If nothing else, you'll get a good laugh when you see management poured out of a bottle.

> Maximum production will never result in maximum profit.

Growth Is Not a Strategy

Go to any major city and you'll see Starbucks. Not a Starbuck, but Starbucks, lots of them. There are eight in Fairfield, where I live, and roughly 90 in San Francisco. There are more than 7,000 in the United States. That's why when I heard Harold Schultz, the CEO of Starbucks, say in an interview, "Growth is not a strategy," I was taken aback.

He's right, and it is a lesson that Starbucks learned the hard way. Starbucks had strayed from their mission: *To inspire and nurture the human spirit—one person, one cup, and one neighborhood at a time.* They increased the number of stores and the products offered at those stores because they could, not because they should. Meanwhile, customer satisfaction fell, profitability declined, and in 2008 and 2009 they closed more than 700 of their coffee shops.

Schultz's observation that growth is not a strategy applies whether we are talking about cups or cows. Expanding an enterprise will not increase profit unless there is a production strategy in place that keeps overheads under control and the gross margin per unit strong.

Starbucks' strategy was to be a place "between work and home" where people could relax, refresh and socialize. Schultz said that they strayed from that mission. As they expanded they diversified their product offering to include sandwiches and other items to increase revenue in each store. It didn't work. As they unintentionally transformed a coffee shop into a restaurant, they lost customers and profits. Schultz said that he knew they were in trouble when he walked into a Starbucks and smelled burned cheese rather than brewed coffee.

Starbucks dropped the sandwiches and returned to its core mission. They closed all of their stores for one day to retrain their 135,000 employees "to pour the perfect shot of espresso." Profits are up and Starbucks has started growing again. This time the growth isn't just for growth's sake. It is to serve more people a great cup of coffee. Growth does not create success. Success creates growth.

• • •

In response to this blog posting, one reader wrote, "When cells in your body grow quickly without organization, they call it cancer. I see a parallel in business growth as well. Successful growth is a carefully planned and orchestrated endeavor with a clearly defined goal, implemented at a sustainable pace."

I think that the cancer analogy is a good one. Unfocused growth is like a cancer. On the other hand, don't think that means slow, steady growth always wins the race either. Planned, organized growth doesn't necessarily mean growth has to be slow. If there is an opportunity for rapid, profitable expansion, we ought to go for it. Growth is often accompanied with growing pains. Sometimes it is best to get them over within a short period rather than draw them out.

Starbucks' problem wasn't so much the pace of growth but that the growth did not support their mission. When an opportunity for explosive growth presents itself, it can be a breakthrough, provided that the growth is consistent with your mission. It can lead to a breakup when it's not.

Another reader seemed to get a message I didn't intend to send when he wrote,

"What a relief. What this and other articles that I have recently read indicate is that if I just concentrate on the important points of raising natural grass-fed beef, all of the other things, including growth, take place."

Whoa! I didn't say that it is enough to produce a great product. It's not. Just because you produce a great product doesn't mean that it is a product people really want, that people will find out about it, that it is priced appropriately, or that it won't have to compete with other great products offered by other people. The point I intended to make is that growth, in and of itself, doesn't necessarily increase profit. I really like the cancer analogy, but (and this is a BIG BUT) that doesn't mean that growth isn't important. It is just that growth must be consistent with your mission and based on a sound business model.

I hope that limited-scale producers don't use this article as an excuse to justify staying small. Having enough scale to cover overheads is essential.

We resist increasing scale because we think it means more work. That's the perspective of an employee, not a business owner. Besides, raising 400 cows is not twice the work of raising 200.

Businesses exist to serve customers and clients. Only by serving them can a business serve the owners. Expansion, when it is consistent with our mission, means we get to deliver more value to more people. Why would we want to limit the number of people we serve?

> Expansion, when it is consistent with our mission, means we get to deliver more value to more people. Why would we want to limit the number of people we serve?

Scale is important. Increasing scale (turnover) is one of the three secrets for increasing profit. It's just that increasing scale must be done in a way that is consistent with your mission.

One Size Doesn't Fit All

We get a cross-section of livestock producers at *The Ranching For Profit School*. Last year we had outfits with more than 10,000 cows and others with less than 100 attend the course. When it comes to enterprise selection and structure, most of the small places look like miniature versions of the large ones. That's a problem because size matters, and what works for the large-scale producers isn't always a good idea for folks working at a smaller scale. One size doesn't fit all.

The primary challenge with limited-scale operations is that they don't have the economies of scale required to maximize the efficiency of their overhead costs. The cost of a pickup truck is the same on a place where one person runs 200 cows as it is on a place where there is one person per 1,000; it's just a lot harder to pay for it with only 200 cows. Since certain overheads are necessary and turnover is constraining, gross margin per unit becomes even more important for smaller-scale producers. If they want to increase profit, smaller-scale producers need to focus on enterprises with the highest margin per unit.

One of the many things limited-scale producers should challenge is their replacement strategy. Like most of their bigger neighbors, most small-scale producers assume they should raise their own replacements. Assuming that a cow/calf enterprise is best suited to their situation (a dangerous assumption), most small-scale producers may be better off not raising their own replacements. The gross margin per standard animal unit (SAU) of heifer enterprises is usually a lot lower than the margin per SAU of the cow herd they support.

There are certain things that people tend to be very sensitive about. Next to our stockmanship, genetics probably tops the list. Most of us take a lot of pride in our eye for quality cattle. Nearly everyone who has cows claims that theirs have superior genetics, and that justifies raising their own replacement heifers. (This claim is similar to the results of a recent survey in which 90% of Americans said they were above-average drivers.) I've been told by geneticists that producers with fewer than 400 cows simply don't have a large enough genetic pool to have an outstanding breeding program. This doesn't mean that it isn't possible to raise quality cattle on a limited scale, but the deck is stacked against it.

It also begs the question, *What is a quality cow?* If it is one that is productive, they may be right in thinking they ought to raise their own replacements. If it is one that is profitable, most of them don't have a leg to stand on.

There are economic realities that every business must face. We must keep overheads low, the margin per unit high and recognize that size matters. If we are limited by scale (a limitation that is usually self-imposed), trying to produce profit by copying the business model of larger-scale neighbors rarely works. One size does not fit all.

• • •

This column sparked a lot of responses about raising heifers. One rancher cut straight to the point, writing, "We like cows and our cows like us, but we have a much higher gross margin with stockers. The only way we can cash flow deeded land is by running stockers."

He makes a great point. The debate to raise or not to raise replacement heifers isn't the primary issue. A prerequisite question is, "Should I have cows?" There are people at workshops and even at *The Ranching For Profit School* who want to know, or at least say they want to know, how to make their cows more efficient. But when we look at their personal objectives, the capabilities of their land and their financial goals, we may find that some of them would go farther faster, and with less expense, if they didn't have cows at all ... and if they should have cows, sometimes they should be someone else's cows. The replacement strategy really doesn't matter if cows are the wrong enterprise in the first place.

Ranching is the business of capturing solar energy through photosynthesis and harvesting it with a four-legged combine. Rather than cow/calf producers or stocker operators, we ought to be thinking of ourselves as sunlight converters. That mindset opens the door to many opportunities. Sheep, anyone?

Another reader wrote, "We have raised our own heifers and purchased heifers, but have found our purchased heifers don't rebreed in our native range. We have had better luck buying three- and four-year-old cows."

He makes another excellent point. Why do we focus on replacement heifers when it is not heifers we need to replace? Perhaps we ought to be talking about replacement cows. With no H2s to calve out, his strategy of using replacement cows probably makes life easier at calving time and dramatically reduces cow depreciation.

Another reader wrote, "We always have to keep in mind the point you have made about whether cow/calf is profitable in the first place, if you are just in the wrong geographic location to start with. Our analysis shows that the low input style is the one thing that makes it possible to ranch here. The big constraint in buying replacement cattle is finding the right ones. I don't think there are very many replacement cattle out there that will make it on our low-input program. Therefore, raising our own replacements might be the only answer and the only way to make the enterprise profitable enough to support itself, let alone pay for extra debt or other inputs."

He raises an important issue. There is definite value to controlling your genetics, and it may be hard to find cattle that will thrive under your program. But the

> To be profitable smaller-scale producers need to focus on enterprises with the highest margin per unit.

question remains, *Is the value of raising your replacements worth the cost?* If you are operating at a limited scale, the answer is usually *No.* Even if half of the "replacement cows" we buy this year are open and are culled out of the herd next year, it may still be more profitable buying replacement cows rather than raising replacement heifers.

There are profitable heifer development programs, but most are run by relatively large outfits. One alumnus who breeds heifers under range conditions with minimal inputs *boasts* a 55% conception rate on H1 heifers. The open heifers go into his feeder program and have a margin nearly as high as the bred heifers. A 55% conception rate might not seem like anything to brag about, but the results are a heifer development program with a healthy gross margin and thrifty cows that are productive under harsh conditions.

One "have your cake and eat it too" alternative for limited-scale producers who feel that they need to control their genetics is to contract with someone else to raise them. This strategy accomplishes three things:

1. They can control their genetics.
2. They don't have to keep low-margin animals on their ranch.
3. It increases their turnover, which, by definition, is the limiting factor for limited-scale producers.

When capacity is limited it is hard to justify having relatively low-margin animals. Of course, if you don't know your enterprise gross margins, decisions regarding enterprise mix and structure can only be based on guesswork and emotion.

The bottom line is that to increase the bottom line, limited-scale operators who want to be profitable face challenges that larger-scale operators don't face. One of those challenges is the need to maximize the gross margin per unit.

Three Questions for Diversification

A lot of people think that diversification increases profit. There are situations where it does, but diversification on many ranches is actually more of a risk management strategy—it eliminates any risk of making a profit! Our benchmarking results show that the most profitable businesses generally have two or three enterprises. Ranches with five or six enterprises are rarely profitable. Generally, the more enterprises someone has, the less profit they make and the more stress they feel.

Nearly every farm or ranch has the potential for several income-generating enterprises. The problem is that not every new enterprise has the potential of producing enough income to justify the time and energy we spend supporting that enterprise. Less profitable enterprises often rob time, energy and space from enterprises that produce more profit.

When you consider diversification, ask yourself three questions:

1. Are we creating a new business or just another job? Unless it is a business, don't do it. The last thing you need is another job.
2. Does it compete with or complement another enterprise? If it competes, it will not increase profit.
3. Can it produce significant income?

One of our alumni says that if an enterprise doesn't have the potential to contribute a gross margin of at least $40,000 per year to his operation, it isn't worth doing. Your target may be different, but there is some minimum needed to make an enterprise worth doing.

If you want to make a profit, concentrate on those things that you do well and do them at scale.

> Doing a lot of small things will wear you out, but it will not increase profit. Highly profitable businesses do just a few things, but they do them in a big way.

193

The Rule of Holes

When you discover you are in a hole, the first thing you should do is stop digging. Of course, most of us figure we probably got in the hole because we weren't working hard enough, so rather than put down the shovel, we dig even faster. China has to be down there someplace.

We assume a breakthrough will come by finding a new market opportunity, restructuring an existing enterprise or exploiting a resource in a way we've overlooked. To find breakthroughs we look for ways to improve the things we are doing or for new things that we can add to our business. But sometimes the simplest and biggest breakthroughs come from stopping things that aren't working. In other words, put down the shovel. Sometimes we make a lot more by doing a lot less.

Every *Ranching For Profit School* alumnus I know who made the leap from below-average returns to benchmark business status (averaging 10% ROA) has one thing in common. Every one of them stopped doing at least one thing that wasn't working. The things that weren't working were different for different businesses. Some were enterprises with a negative margin. Others were enterprises that required huge divisional overheads or tied up a disproportionate share of capital. By discontinuing the things that didn't work, they had more capital available for the things that did work, they had more carrying capacity for their profitable enterprises and they had more free time.

The 80/20 rule says that 80% of the things we do produce 20% of the results. That means that 20% of the things we do produce 80% of the results. Just imagine swapping those proportions, focusing 80% of your time on things that produce 80% of the result!

Let's say we work 100 hours to produce an income of $1,000. If the 80/20 rule is true then we spent 80 hours producing $200 ($2.50/hour) and 20 hours producing $800 ($40/hour). The impact of shifting our priorities is staggering. If we take 80% of our time on the high-yielding task ($40/hour) and only 20% of our time on the low-return work ($2.50/hour), our income would be $3,250! Of course, rather than swap the proportions, it makes even more sense to put down the shovel and completely stop the low-return work.

> When you find yourself in a hole, stop digging.

Wealthy on the Balance Sheet and Broke at the Bank

- Can Cows Pay for the Ranch?

- Facing the 900-Pound Gorilla

- Getting Started in Ranching

- Thirteen Pointers for Profit

Can Cows Pay for the Ranch?

I had a call from an alumnus considering a big move. He was thinking of selling his place and relocating. He had his eyes on a property in another state and asked me, "Can the cash flow generated from a cow/calf operation make the land payments?"

As a general rule, I figure a cow can pay about one-and-a-half times her value for the land it takes to support her. If we figure that the average value of a cow is about $1,000, the positive cash flow she generates, assuming she has a decent gross margin, should cover the land payment for $1,500 worth of property. If it takes 10 acres to carry a cow, that means the value for grazing is $150 an acre. Good luck finding that! Of course, if your gross margin is above average you can afford to pay a little more. If your gross margin is below average you'd better improve it before you think about buying land or getting any more cows.

The land he was considering was priced at $600 per acre, with a carrying capacity of about 10 acres per cow. It would require about $6,000 of land to support one cow. Using the "1.5 x Cow Value" rule, that is roughly four times what he can afford to pay, based on the annual income from a cow/calf enterprise. The land isn't necessarily overvalued, it is just overvalued for grazing. Water, minerals, wildlife, the scenery and other attributes of the property all contribute to its overall value.

People who buy ranches often cite the long-term appreciation of the land as the rationale for the investment. But appreciation won't create the cash flow needed to make the payments. If we want the purchase of a ranch to work financially, we need to look for ways to capitalize or concessionize the values associated with the property. Concessionizing means developing an enterprise to create income from

> A cow can pay about one-and-a-half times her value for the land that it takes to support her.

an unused resource. Capitalizing means divesting yourself of a resource you don't intend to use (e.g., selling an easement).

If we capitalize some assets and create some income from other enterprises, the cows won't have to make the whole land payment themselves. In this case, there wasn't anything obvious that could be capitalized or concessionized that would make a significant difference.

Some of our alumni have used cell grazing to dramatically increase the carrying capacity of their ranches. If this rancher is able to double the carrying capacity, instead of one-quarter of the land payment, income from grazing may be able to comfortably make one-half of the payment.

But be cautious. I warn people about being overly optimistic about the improvement they will make through cell grazing. I advised the caller that if he thinks he can increase the capacity by 100%, pencil in a 50% increase. After all, while you can make an educated guess about the potential, you won't really know how much the capacity will increase until you have actually increased it. Even then, unless you can point to areas that are currently underutilized, you shouldn't increase the stocking rate until you've increased the capacity, and that may take a few years. In the meantime, you still have a land payment to make.

There are often compelling, non-economic reasons for buying land. Perhaps it helps consolidate holdings, simplifies the operation or provides security, protecting the rest of the property. These are all good reasons to consider a purchase, but let's not kid ourselves. Even with cell grazing, the price of land is usually well above the value of the grass. However, capitalizing or concessionizing resources, combined with cell grazing, can make buying a ranch a smart financial move.

Facing the 900-Pound Gorilla

Most land-owning ranchers are wealthy on their balance sheet and broke in their bank account. Most operate at an economic loss and survive only because they subsidize the ranch with off-farm income or work without paying themselves. One reason for the poor profitability is the heavy investment most ranchers have in fixed assets. Simply put, fixed assets are things we intend to keep, like land, machinery, vehicles and cows.

If you have any doubt that a cow is a fixed asset, ask yourself, "Do I hope that the whole herd shows up dry and open so I can cull them all this year?" You probably hope that they are all wet and pregnant so you can keep them. Cows are fixed assets.

Working capital includes things we intend to sell, like calves. The massive investment in fixed assets required by conventional ranching is the biggest financial problem in ranching. After all, if all of your money is tied up in things you intend to keep, you'll have very little left to sell to generate income. Making things even worse, a high proportion of your meager income will probably be spent maintaining those fixed assets.

When is an asset a liability?

Your accountant puts fixed assets on the asset side of your balance sheets. Robert Kiyosaki disagrees. In his best-selling book *Rich Dad, Poor Dad*, Kiyosaki defines assets as things that make you money, and liabilities as things that cost you money. Fixed assets cost you money because of the costs required to maintain them. While the accountant is right to call these things assets, Kiyosaki is right too, because keeping a high proportion of your money tied up in fixed assets is a liability to a business. It is ironic that the things that symbolize wealth in our culture (fixed assets) impede our capacity to create wealth.

There are three choices:
1. Maintain the status quo and continue to keep the bulk of your wealth tied up in nonproductive assets.
2. Capitalize (sell) the fixed assets.
3. Concessionize the asset to create an ongoing stream of income.

In the case of machinery, these three options could be:

Choice	Action	Result
1. Status quo	Keep the tractor.	Low ROA. Capital locked up. Low cash flow.
2. Capitalize	Sell the tractor.	Free the capital currently locked up in the tractor.
3. Concessionize	Rent the tractor or custom farm.	Higher ROA. Cash flow increased.

At *The Ranching For Profit School* I often ask people to make a list of all the resources that contribute to the value of their ranches. I then ask them to work with one another to brainstorm options for either divesting themselves of unproductive assets or putting those assets to work. It is important that they discuss this with their tablemates, because it is almost always easier to find ways that someone *else* can capitalize or concessionize *their* fixed assets.

Ranching is the management of all ranch resources, including the minerals below it, the water flowing across it, the grass growing on it, the wildlife passing through it, the wind blowing over it and even the scenery as we look beyond it.

Common examples of capitalizing are selling the mineral rights and selling easements.

We have alumni who have concessionized assets by developing wind, gravel and recreation enterprises. One *Executive Link* member composts manure in his bison feedlot, then produces and packages compost tea that is sold in high-end nurseries. He has concessionized his bison poop resource.

No one has to do anything they don't want to do provided they can afford it. But many ranchers can't afford to continue ignoring the cost of sitting on high-value assets without earning a return from those assets.

You might think that capitalizing and concessionizing are just fancy names for finding ways to subsidize the ranch. They are not. There is a major difference between subsidizing the ranch and capitalizing or concessionizing ranch resources.

Capitalizing and concessionizing take advantage of unused or underutilized ranch assets that already contribute to the overall value of the property. By definition, subsidizing is supporting the ranch with income that is unrelated to the ranch resources. None of the examples of capitalizing or concessionizing that I've described are subsidizing the ranch any more than adding a custom grazing enterprise to take advantage of extra forage and your management skills (both ranch resources). If you are in the livestock AND the land business and need to increase profit from your ranch, you probably need to start thinking about using more than just grass.

• • •

In a workshop in which I cited several examples of how *Ranching For Profit School* alumni had capitalized and concessionized assets, a participant said that he wasn't interested in knowing what people were doing outside the livestock industry to make money. He said, "I want to know how to be more profitable with livestock. Period." That's simple enough. Reduce the overheads, improve the gross margin per unit and increase the turnover. But that may not be profitable enough if you own or are buying ranch land.

If you own your land, if the market value of your land is way out of line with the value of the grass, and if you need to increase profit, you need to think about ways to capitalize or concessionize those other values. That might not be the *livestock* business, but it *is* ranching. When we think about ranch management we ought to think about management of all of a ranch's resources. Those resources may include the minerals below it, the water flowing across it, the grass growing on it, the wildlife passing through it, the wind blowing over it and even the scenery as we look beyond it. Land owners who are not considering how these values can be capitalized or concessionized are ignoring the 900-pound gorilla in the room.

• • •

After benchmarking all of our *Executive Link* businesses, I ran several "what if" scenarios with the data. In one scenario, I zeroed out the value of the land and property tax payments and entered in a value for market rent. When I did that, the return on assets (ROA) benchmark shot up from 8% to 13%. (The benchmark for businesses that actually own no land was 23% ROA.) That shows that the livestock business can be very profitable. It also suggests what you already know to be true—that ranches are overvalued for grazing and that most ranchers are not doing much to harvest the multitude of other things that drive the value of their land.

We make the assumption that capitalizing or concessionizing will somehow infringe on our lifestyle. But take a closer look. There are probably some assets that could be capitalized or concessionized in ways that are consistent with your values, and that would enrich your life *and* your bank account.

Getting Started in Ranching

A few years ago I was invited to participate in a workshop sponsored by a County Cattlemen's Association meeting in eastern Oregon. Prior to my program there was an Extension Service meeting with several presenters. An economist made a Power-Point presentation using graphs and tables to show the economic impact of ranches to the region. In the Q&A period, an older gentleman in the audience asked, "Given the high capital costs involved in getting into ranching, how does a young person get started?" He went on to say that given the aging population of ranchers in the area and the economic barrier young people face in getting started, the economic benefit to the region might evaporate before too long.

The response from the economist was telling. In answer to how a young person could get started in ranching he said, "It would be really hard." Then he said, "An off-farm job would help." He had nothing more to say on that topic.

He's right of course, it is tough. But I immediately thought of *Ranching For Profit School* alumni who have successfully tackled that issue. Realizing that the land and livestock businesses are two separate entities is the first step. Using this knowledge, they've realized that unless they have generous parents with deep pockets or they are satisfied to work for someone else, there are only two strategies young people can use to get started.

The first strategy is not to own any fixed assets. This was the strategy used by Rex and Brad Radtke. They developed a custom grazing business on rented land. Brad told me that when they started, the only things the business owned were an old pickup truck and a four wheeler. An established business may be able to get away with having more fixed assets, although they'll likely have a lower ROA. Owning lots of "things" can be an impossible barrier to success if you are just starting out.

The other strategy is to own only the portion of the fixed assets you intend to use. This is the strategy that a young couple in Oregon used to buy their ranch. They put together a group of "conservation investors" who wanted to invest in a property that was being managed to improve the ecosystem. The investor agreement is clear. The couple has full control over all resource and ranch management decisions. Using the capital they generated, they were able to make the down payment. Then they used a conservation easement to divest themselves of the development value of the property. Essentially they just own the grass, and the cattle enterprise is profitable enough to pay for that.

Both of these strategies are easier said than done. For every person I've met who has successfully developed an operation around either of these principles, I know one who hasn't been able to make it work. Things almost always cost more and take longer than it seems they should. For example, it only took the Oregon couple six weeks to find the investors, but it took nearly *two years* to finalize the conservation easement.

> Part of success is creating the right business model. Part of it is an absolute commitment to succeeding. Part of it boils down to being in the right place at the right time.

Part of success is creating the right business model. Part of it is an absolute commitment to succeeding. And some of it boils down to being in the right place at the right time.

The Extension Service guy was right. It is tough, and it will require people with brains and determination to succeed. That's good news. Tomorrow's ranchers will have to be smarter and more determined than ever. I wonder what kind of answers they will demand from the Extension Service.

Thirteen Pointers for Profit

The livestock business can be a very profitable business. Using the beginning herd value as the asset value, there are many *Ranching For Profit School* alumni earning double-digit returns from livestock after paying rent, their salaries, interest and all production-related costs. Here are my observations about what they have in common:

1. They fit the enterprise to the resource. You can cram a square peg into a round hole, but it will cost you. Carrying cows year-round in country where the snow is up to your eyeballs for four months probably isn't a good fit to the environment.
2. They minimize capital investment.
3. They eliminate nearly all the overheads (except rent and salaries).
4. They don't try to starve a profit into the business. They expect a lot from labor and they reward labor well. They realize that it usually isn't ineffective labor that results in poor profit, but ineffective management. It doesn't matter if labor is doing things right if management has them doing the wrong things.
5. They run at scale so that labor effectiveness is maximized. Stan Parsons used to talk about 1,000 cows per employee. Many of our Australian alumni run well over that.
6. They feed supplements but don't feed substitutes. Supplemental feeding makes up for deficiencies in quality (e.g., minerals and protein). Substitute feeding makes up for deficiencies in quantity (e.g., energy). If they haven't completely eliminated hay, the most profitable ranches feed less than 1/4 ton per cow.

7. They let nature do most of the work. They use nature as a role model, and if they run cows, they calve in sync with the grass.

8. They project their margins and work on strategies to improve profit BEFORE the year even starts. Rather than try to minimize inputs or maximize production, they focus on optimizing the margin. Once the year starts, they track their actuals, compare them to their projections, and make adjustments to stay on course.

9. They don't farm to support their livestock. Very few ranchers farm at the scale necessary to make a profit from farming. Farming includes hay making.

10. If they are cow/calf producers they understand that their profitability is driven by the cull cow business. They improve the margin on their cows (and culls) by minimizing cow depreciation. Most add value to their culls and either buy their replacements or find a low-cost solution to the high cost of raising their own replacements.

11. They stop doing things that don't work. While that may sound obvious, I'm always struck by how many people continue enterprises that have negative gross margins or that grossly underperform. Most people try to fix things that don't work, and that's okay, but it is often more profitable and less stressful to discontinue them and focus on the things that are already working.

12. They aren't greedy and don't roll the dice trying to hit the top of the market. They are willing to take a modest profit early and often, especially if it conserves their grass.

13. They are excellent grass managers

While these things may be enough to make the livestock business profitable, the question remains as to whether it is enough to make *your* ranch profitable. In most areas the market value of land is far above the value of the grass. Profitable ranching requires the management of *all* of the ranch's resources and values, not just the grass.

> If the market value of your land is way out of line with the value of the grass, trying to increase profit by making your livestock operation more efficient is like trying to raft the Colorado River at flood stage in an inner tube.

Trying to make a ranch profitable solely by making the livestock operation more efficient is like trying to raft the Colorado River at flood stage in an inner tube. You will be well advised to think of how to capitalize or concessionize those other values.

The Best Laid Plans

- Coveting Thy Neighbor's Land

- A False Opportunity

- Working Backwards

- Are You Afraid of the Dark?

- The Hardest Part of Change Is Changing

- Regret That You Did or Didn't

- The Best Kept Secret in Ranching

Coveting Thy Neighbor's Land

At a recent *Executive Link* meeting a member asked her board for help with a decision that had been troubling her. The ranch needed to increase its land base to increase turnover. The question she asked her board was, *Should I buy the land or rent the land?*

At *The Ranching for Profit School* we show people how owning fixed assets like land will generally decrease the economic efficiency of an enterprise. Stan Parsons underscored the difference between the land business and the livestock business and stressed that the *cows must rent the ranch.* Allan Nation frequently writes about not having to own land to ranch. Greg Judy tells a great story in his book *No Risk Ranching* about making money with no fixed assets. With all of this in mind, the *Executive Link* board started to work on the problem and crunch the numbers. Sure enough, their calculations showed that the cattle enterprise would not be able to make the land payments, let alone make a profit. End of discussion? Not quite.

There's an important question everyone almost forgot to ask: *What do you want to do?* While the economics and finances of the situation showed that she'd be better off to lease, deep down she wanted to buy. The property provided protection from potential development, increased the convenience of the existing operation, and would help her sleep better at night. What's all that worth?

The question should not have been, *Should I buy or lease?* The question should have been, *How can I make buying this land a good economic decision?* It took only three minutes focused on this new question before the board found several ways to buy the land, cover the payments and make a profit.

The *Ranching For Profit* paradigm is still the minority paradigm in the livestock industry, but when we hang around people who share the same paradigm, we run the danger of experiencing "group think." When everyone starts thinking the same way, no one is thinking very much.

Remember, you aren't producing grass and livestock to impress Stan or Allan or me. You ought not try to be Greg Judy. Let Greg be Greg. Learn what you can from the story each of us has to tell. But we don't have to live with you, your spouse, your kids, your conscience or your banker. You do. Determine what you want and then find a way to do it.

> When everyone starts thinking the same way, no one is thinking very much.

A False Opportunity

In a workshop discussion on setting economic and financial targets, one participant told me that he found it hard to set targets and that if he could just make a little *more* each year, *someday* he'd be satisfied. While we may not phrase it quite the way he did, his approach is the way most of us go about trying to improve our situations. We are so busy working we find it hard to set targets and create a plan to achieve them. But meaningful targets are important. To be meaningful, economic targets must include both a measurable number and specific date. The problem with the workshop participant's approach is that "more" is not a number and "someday" is not a time.

Without a profit target people tend to follow false opportunities. For example, we think that if we add one small opportunity after another we'll eventually "make it." But the opposite is often true.

For example, renting pasture is probably the most common and most tempting false opportunity. In most places it is tough to lease land, so our tendency is to jump at any leases that are available. But by taking on every lease that becomes available, we may become so busy and be stretched so thin that we kill ourselves, if not physically and financially, then emotionally and spiritually.

The worst part is that the time and resources we invest in false opportunities may distract us from finding the breakthrough that could have made a real difference, something that would enable us to run 500 more cows, or 1,000.

> The time and resources we invest in false opportunities may distract us from finding the breakthrough that could make a real difference.

Of course, increasing capacity by leasing pasture is vital for many ranchers. But rather than jumping at every lease that becomes available, I recommend to our clients that they list the criteria they will use to judge the opportunity. For example:

✓ What is the minimum capacity that would make it worthwhile?

✓ What is the maximum distance from home? (This will probably depend on the carrying capacity of the lease.)

✓ What is the minimum gross margin it must contribute to your business?

Perhaps you can achieve your life and business goals with 100 cows. Maybe it will take 1,000 or maybe 10,000. Maybe you should own them, maybe not. Maybe it can't be done with cows. I don't know what it will take to achieve your goals. The problem is, unless you have clearly defined your goals and have translated them into measurable targets, you don't know either.

• • •

In response to this column one reader wrote, "I understand the principle, you can spread yourself too thin and not be effective. My question is what do you do in the time between? Do we not take the 'opportunities' that come along until we get the chance to hit our big goal? Do we go get a job in town to make ends meet? Is it better to sit on the sideline and wait, or do we keep pushing through? I have found that I have made a lot of mistakes through the little 'opportunities' further away from home, but these are where I learned a lot of the things that I needed to learn. Many times these are the areas that create the breakthrough that we were after to begin with. Definitely, the older I get the less I want to have these false opportunities."

The answer to this, and to most of the questions I get (and all *Ranching For Profit School* alumni know this is my favorite answer) is, "It depends." The point is to have a picture of where you want to be and a pretty good idea of the path that will take you there. If the so-called opportunity you are considering doesn't take you closer and consumes time, energy and money that could be used to make progress, then don't take it. If it is consistent with your goal and moves you closer to it, then go for it. It's just that some things that initially look like opportunities turn out to be rabbit trails. You need to have a clear long-term vision to be able to tell if the opportunity puts you on the right path or leads you down a dead-end trail.

One *Executive Link* member added: "One of my action steps for the summer *Executive Link* meeting was to come up with a 10-year plan. I agonized over this seemingly daunting task. How much do you lay out? How specific should it be? I almost felt guilty about how simple the plan I came up with turned out. All I did was set yearly profit targets from now until 2021. Everything we do from now until 2021 will be driven by those targets. We will be guided by our mission statement and values along the way to make sure our compass is always due north. It really is that simple. I don't have any illusions about how complicated actual day-to-day operations will be, but I know where we are headed."

There is a lesson here for all of us: set simple goals that work within your framework of core values. This approach will help you achieve your long term goals and avoid false opportunities.

Working Backwards

I've been getting a lot of emails lately like this: "I've only got 40 cows. Is it worthwhile for me to come to *The Ranching For Profit School*?" They know that our program is focused on people serious about building a sustainable livestock business and that, with rare exception, 40 beef cows is usually more of a hobby than a business.

It's not surprising that I get a lot of those calls. Eighty percent of producers raising beef cows in the United States and Canada have fewer than 50 cows. They account for 30% of the total number of beef cows in our two countries. And I suppose it isn't surprising that most of us tend to focus on what we have (in this case, 40 cows). After all, that's what we see and work with every day.

But it really doesn't matter what you have. What matters is what you *want*. Once we identify what we want, we need to ask what we need to do to get it.

Whether developing the annual operating plan or a strategic plan that describes your ultimate goal and the enterprises that will support it, economic planning is not about numbers. It's about policies and practices. Don't start by asking how much you will spend or how many cows you will cull this year. Start by asking how old the herd is, what the forage conditions are, and how you plan to supplement the animals to get the performance you need. Develop policies and tactics first, then translate them into numbers of animals and finally into dollars. When you are *Ranching For Profit* the *planning* is more important than the plan!

> "In preparing for battle I've always found that plans are useless, but planning is indispensable."
> Dwight D. Eisenhower

The Ranching For Profit economic model works like this:
1. Breeding herd statistics chart (projects reproductive performance rates)
2. Stock flow plan (projects sales, purchases, and closing inventory)
3. Livestock valuation (shows the value of our inventory)
4. Trading account (shows the value produced by an enterprise)
5. Cash flow (forecasts income, direct costs, overheads and capital expenses, and shows periods of cash surplus and deficit)
6. Enterprise gross margin (shows the economic efficiency of an enterprise)
7. Profit and loss account (combines all enterprise gross margins and deducts the overhead costs to project profit or loss)

Step by step, it is a very simple and effective model, but it is backwards! Too often we run the numbers from beginning to end to see what will be left over and determine if something will work. We'd be well advised to work the process backwards, starting with the end in mind. Determine a profit target, then see what you have to do to achieve it:
1. Set a profit target.
2. Challenge every overhead cost. Then add the overheads you will incur to the profit target. This is the total gross margin you will need to cover your overheads and achieve your profit target (your gross margin target).
3. Determine the gross margin that each enterprise must contribute to the total and the gross margin per unit, and the number of units you'll need in each enterprise to hit those targets.

4. Work through the stock flow and the breeding herd statistics chart to determine what level of performance you'll need to achieve in order to make the business successful.

Whether planning for the production year or for the decade, you'll find that beginning with the end is a much more powerful way to produce the results you want. To move your business forward, sometimes you need to work backward.

Are You Afraid of the Dark?

Why are people afraid of the dark? Probably because they don't know what's out there. Is it really the dark that scares them, or is it the unknown lurking in the dark? When you think about it this way it is clear: we are afraid of the unknown.

The same is true for changes we may be contemplating in our ranches. It's not the change that scares us. It is the unknown impacts that the change may bring that can paralyze us. The tools we teach in *The Ranching For Profit School* are designed to help ranchers make the unknown more known and take the fear out of change.

When Alberta rancher Cam Gardner took *The Ranching For Profit School*, the school was a day longer than it is now. We arranged a field trip on that day to visit a ranch that was applying cell grazing principles. (We stopped doing the trip because standing out in the middle of a pasture when it's 20° below zero and the wind is howling wasn't as much fun as it sounds.) Cam decided not to go on the trip. It wasn't just to stay warm in the classroom; he wanted to work on his numbers. When I got back to the classroom he was still sitting there. I don't think he had budged. He was surrounded by pages of calculations he had made, and some of them were crumpled up on the floor. He looked stressed.

When I asked what was wrong, he told me that his calculations showed that the ranch was losing money, but that by applying the concepts he'd learned in the class, it looked as though they could make a good profit. Thinking that having a profitable solution should be good news, I asked, "What's the problem then?"

"Garbage in, garbage out!" he said. "I don't have any confidence in my figures."

I asked him how far off he thought his estimates might be. "Could they be off by 50%?" I asked. He said, "No. I'm not that far off."

I asked if they might be off by 20%. He didn't think so.

"Could they be off by 10%?" He said they might be. So, in addition to using conservative performance estimates, we knocked 10% off of all his cattle sales and added 10% to all of his direct costs. The result was still better than the status quo. That took a lot of the fear out of making the change.

In Cam's case it wasn't necessary, but as long as we are going to look at the worst-case scenario, we ought to also project a best-case scenario to see if the upside of change is attractive enough to warrant taking some risk. While we ought not bank on the best case, we can improve our odds by asking ourselves what steps we can take to make the best case more likely.

We all have a lot of options available to us, whether it is in the type of enterprises we run or in the way we structure those enterprises. But even when the status quo isn't very profitable, we often stick with it because the unknowns of the alternatives scare us even more. We can't tell if they lead to danger or opportunity until we shine some light on those unknowns. We will never see the future with 20/20 vision, but the *Ranching For Profit* tools (e.g., stock flow, cash flow, enterprise gross margin projections) can help you make the unknown more known and take a lot of the fear out of the future.

Surgery with a chain saw

People who like precision aren't always comfortable with making projections. Since we don't know exactly how many calves we will wean, how many cows we will cull, how dry it will be, what markets will do and what prices we will pay, every number we enter may be wrong. I tell people in *The Ranching*

For Profit School that when you are looking for deadwood in a business, do surgery with a chain saw, not a scalpel. If you think $10,000 is the difference between a good year and a bad year, you are mistaken. It was never going to be a good year.

The answer to uncertainty is to project the gross margin and profitability of alternative scenarios. None of them may be precise, but with a little thought they ought to be accurate enough to provide useful information. The *planning* is usually more valuable than the plan.

> People don't fear change.
> They fear the unknown.
> Planning can take a lot of
> the unknown out of change.

The Hardest Part of Change is Changing

When my wife, Kathy, was pregnant with our first child, we took childbirth classes. Among other things, we learned about the different phases of labor. The first stage of labor is divided into two parts:

1. Early labor, where the cervix gradually thins out and dilates.
2. Active labor, where the cervix dilates more rapidly and contractions are longer, stronger, and closer together. The last part of active labor is often called transition. This is the part where your sweet, loving wife asks for drugs and says things you are happy your soon-to-be-born child isn't around to hear yet.

The nurse warned us that transition would be the toughest part of the birthing process. Transition is also the toughest part of implementing change.

I spoke to a rancher who said he was considering changing his calving season to eliminate the need for hay. He had been calving in March and told me he was going to shift it to early April next year. The next year he thought he'd change it by a few more weeks. Ultimately, four or five years from now, he figured he'd wind up in late May or early June. That's what he felt the ideal calving season would be for his area. I agree, but I couldn't disagree more with the way he is planning to make the change. He should make the jump to May/June calving as quickly as he can.

Until he gets the calving season moved to where it needs to be, he will have nearly all the costs of the old way of doing things and very few of the advantages of the new way.

The hardest part of change is the changing! The angst of change comes during the transition. One reason we tend to implement change slowly is that we aren't sure the new way is going to work. Unfortunately, changing slowly rarely gives us an effective test of the advantages of the new strategy. It is why we often see poorer results during the transition period than we get from either the old way or the new way.

The solution to uncertainty isn't to take half measures or to transition slowly. It is to do more research to remove as many of the unknowns as possible before taking the plunge! It helps to run some pessimistic scenarios of the new strategy. If they turn out to be better than the status quo, it takes a lot of the fear out of change. Once we've determined that the change is the right thing to do, we will get better results and feel less stress if we minimize the transition period.

> The hardest part of change is the changing! You will achieve more success faster by determining the right strategy, committing to it, and making the transition to it as short as possible.

I once heard Jim Hightower, a former Texas agriculture commissioner, say that the only things in the middle of the road are yellow stripes and dead armadillos. When it comes to building a sustainable business, you will achieve more success faster by determining the right strategy, committing to it, and making the transition to it as short as possible. The alternative may make you a flattened armadillo.

Regret That You Did or Didn't

It's no news to any of you that we've had several dryer than "normal" years in the past decade. Some are suggesting that these conditions are the new normal. Only time will tell whether or not that's true. But one thing is for sure: as you drive down rural roads, it's pretty easy to tell who knows how to manage in drought and who doesn't.

There is no substitute for destocking. If you have only half the supply, you'd better have only half the demand. Having an enterprise mix compatible with the drought risk makes implementing this cardinal rule of good drought management easier.

It is also essential to identify a critical rain date. That's the date by which, if it hasn't rained, you know you are in trouble. That date is the trigger for implementing your destocking plan.

A few years ago, Kansas rancher and friend Pete Ferrell was telling me about a dry spell he'd experienced. He said, "I hit our critical rain date and I still hadn't had any rain, so I destocked. By the middle of June, all of the animals were gone." Then it started to rain. He said that it turned out to be a very unusual summer with a good soaking rain nearly every week for the rest of the season. It turned out that he had a decent forage year after all.

Pete said he could have made more profit if he hadn't destocked when he did, but he still came out all right. If he hadn't had an unusual summer, not destocking could have had negative impacts on the land that he might have felt for years. Then Pete said something that he'd heard Stan Parsons say years earlier. He said, "I figure there are two types of regret in our lives: regret for the things we did and regret for the things we didn't do."

> "There are two types of regret in our lives: regret for the things we did and regret for the things we didn't do."
> Stan Parsons

Provided we've done our due diligence and things have passed muster, the regrets for the things we've done generally pale in comparison to the regrets for the things we didn't do.

The Best Kept Secret in Ranching

Yesterday I called a rancher from Oklahoma who had requested information about our programs. When I mentioned *The Ranching For Profit School* he scoffed, "Ranching for profit! That's an oxymoron." Looking at the environment in which we operate, it's easy to draw that conclusion. Since 1970, input costs have increased five times faster than cattle prices. We all know what's happened to land values. And now with credit difficulties, it's not hard to see why someone would think it is impossible to make a profit in ranching.

But the fact is that there are profitable ranches. They have a wide variety of enterprises in a diversity of environments. Some are first-generation ranches while others have been at it for more than 100 years. They include relatively small ranches and some of the largest ranches in the world. The most rewarding part of owning and running Ranch Management Consultants has been to work with forward-thinking ranchers from every ranching state and province. There's nothing that compares to seeing the light-bulb turn on for someone in class and walking with them in their pastures as they talk excitedly about the changes they are seeing. Maybe the best part is spending an evening with them as they talk about the transformation they've seen in their land, their lives and their businesses. While they may not recognize it, the biggest transformation of all is in themselves.

> If someone is doing it, it must be possible.

These uncommon people share some common characteristics:

1. They work *ON* their business (WOTB), regularly.
2. They know their numbers and they know what their numbers mean.

3. They work on their relationships.
4. They structure their operation so nature does the heavy lifting. Their job is to help nature do what comes naturally.

These things don't guarantee that you'll make a profit, but if you want to make a profit you'd be well advised to do these four things.

The best kept secret in ranching? Ranching *can* be profitable. After all, if it is being done (and many of our alumni *are* doing it), it is possible!

Conclusion

Eating an Elephant

I received an email from someone who works for a resource conservation district in the northeastern U.S. who participated in one of our first *Ranching For Profit* webinars. He shared his frustration with the difficulty of helping people improve their land and their lives. He wrote, "I can't tell you how empty I feel sometimes trying to get folks to change their mindset." He ran through a list of relatively simple things people could do, that wouldn't cost any money, that would improve their pastures and increase their profit.

I empathize with his frustration. If misery loves company then he'll be ecstatic, because he isn't alone in finding that changing the way people think is a challenge. MIT's Peter Senge wrote, "What makes learning something new so difficult is not the new ideas but giving up the old ideas." Stan Parsons, who created *The Ranching For Profit School*, always told me that the primary purpose of the school, and our most difficult challenge, was "to challenge people's paradigms."

Asking how you change the widely held paradigms in agriculture is akin to asking, "How do you eat an elephant?" The answer of course is, "One bite at a time." I suggested to the person who sent me the email that if he can find one or two people who are receptive to his ideas, he should devote his energies to helping them make their "breakthrough." As he approaches them, I hope he'll be careful about how he packages those ideas. I'm guessing that the harder he pushes, the fewer people he'll attract. The last person people want to be around is a born-again grazier. I think he'll teach people more by asking them questions than by giving them answers.

As I read the email, I thought about the 14 years I spent facing similar challenges as a Livestock and Range Management Advisor with the University of California. I used my leave and took leave without pay to teach *Ranching For Profit Schools* for Stan. I felt that I had more impact teaching one *Ranching For Profit School* than I had in one year with the University. When I left the University to assume leadership of Ranch Management Consultants, I felt I had done my best, but I was also disappointed that I hadn't made more of an impact.

> "What makes learning something new so difficult is not the new ideas but giving up the old ideas."
> Peter Senge

Then something happened that caused me to question the true impact I may have had. I attended a ranch tour that included a presentation by a very successful grazier in a neighboring county. He gets paid to graze. About one-third of his income comes from grazing other people's properties with his animals. He gave a compelling presentation. At the end of the tour, as we were getting on the bus to leave, I thanked him for sharing his time and experience with us so generously, and I asked, "Where did you get the idea to do what you are doing?" He looked at me and said, "I got it from you!" He had attended a one-day cell grazing workshop I'd held 20 years earlier. I barely remembered the workshop. As I recall, there were only a handful of people there, so I had not considered the workshop a success.

I believe that transforming agriculture is just like eating an elephant. Agriculture will change one farm or ranch at a time. Let's start with yours.

RMC Programs

Changing Agriculture One Business at a Time

Read the popular press about ranching or spend much time in the coffee shop and you'll hear that the glass is half empty. Prices are too low. If they're high, it won't last. Politicians and agencies can't be trusted. Environmentalists are out to get you! Ninety-eight percent of the people in this country no longer have a direct connection to agriculture. It's getting warmer and dryer, and if it happens to be wet, the next drought is not far away.

Whether these things are true or not is irrelevant. There's no point complaining about things you can't do anything about. At Ranch Management Consultants we believe that it isn't the situation but what you do about it that counts. After all, this is the environment in which you choose to do business. That's right, you have a choice. You can choose to quit and do something else, or you can choose to stay. If you choose the latter, you are accepting that the business, political, social and physical environments that exist are the ones you have to navigate. *The Ranching For Profit School* and *Executive Link* are intended to help you plot your course through an undeniably challenging environment to a brighter future.

The Ranching For Profit School

The Ranching For Profit School is a one-week business school for farmers and ranchers. The objective of the course is to help participants transform their ranches into sustainable businesses. Topics include economics, finance, improving the effectiveness of family business relationships, ecology, grazing, livestock production and much more. Throughout the course, whether we are discussing

> "Hands down, this is the best investment we have ever made in our business."
> *Clint Olson, Oklahoma*

cell grazing, soil health, supplementation or reproduction, we are also looking at the impact these have on gross margin, turnover, overheads cost, cash flow and our capital investment.

Each *Ranching For Profit* participant takes home a prioritized action plan showing what needs to be done, who is accountable for doing it and the deadline by which it will be achieved.

The school has helped thousands of ranchers on four continents increase profit, improve the health of their land and build a secure future for their families.

Executive Link

Executive Link helps *Ranching For Profit School* alumni turn their great ideas into positive actions. It provides the structure, support, objective analysis and the accountability it takes to be successful.

Executive Link members are teamed with other *Ranching For Profit School* alumni in peer advisory boards. Boards meet three times a year in facilitated meetings to review each member's business. The *Executive Link* program also includes an outstanding continuing education program designed to challenge your thinking and keep you moving forward. It includes benchmarking software and step-by-step assignments to implement *Ranching For Profit* principles.

> "Taking the school and joining Executive Link is the most rewarding investment our family has ever made. Every dollar spent has been returned 50 times in hard currency and quality of life."
> Cam Gardner, Alberta

For more information about *The Ranching For Profit School* and *Executive Link*, please contact Ranch Management Consultants, Inc.

Phone: (707) 429-2292
Email: rmc@ranchmanagement.com
Website: www.ranchingforprofit.com

Glossary

Terms Used in Section 1: Healthy Land

Biodiversity — The variety of life forms, the genes they contain, and the ecosystems they form.

Carrying Capacity — The total forage produced in an area and available for grazing. It is usually measured by the number of animals that an area can potentially support for a year (e.g., one cow per 20 acres).

Cell Grazing — A grazing management method that:
1. Allows appropriate recovery after grazing for plants
2. Keeps graze periods short to improve animal performance
3. Uses high stock density to uniformly graze paddocks
4. Matches the stocking rate (forage demand) to the carrying capacity (forage supply)
5. Uses herd effect as needed

Feed Banking — Forage that has been accumulated during the growing season for use during a slow growth or dormant season.

Graze Period — The length of time animals spend in a paddock before being moved to another. In cell grazing, graze periods are usually relatively short (one to seven days).

Grazing Cell — An area managed for grazing as a unit. A grazing cell usually consists of many paddocks.

H1 — An H1 is a weaned heifer calf that will be exposed to the bull.

H2 — When an H1 is confirmed pregnant, it becomes an H2. An H2 becomes a cow after it has had its first calf and is confirmed pregnant for the second time.

Herd Effect — The physical impact on soil and vegetation from a herd of animals. It includes chipping capped soil, trampling vegetation, and depositing dung and urine.

Paddock — A division within a grazing cell in which livestock graze.

Rest or Recovery Period — The time livestock are kept out of a paddock. The appropriate rest period changes during the season and depends on the rate of pasture growth.

Stocking Rate — The forage demand of grazing animals. We measure stocking rate using Stock Days per Acre (SDA).

Stock Days Per Acre (SDA) — A measure of stocking rate. It is calculated by multiplying the number of animals in a herd by the days they grazed an area, divided by the acres in that area.

Stock Density — The number of animals per acre in a paddock at a particular moment. For example, if a herd of 400 head grazes a 50-acre paddock, the stock density is eight head per acre.

Stockpiled Forage — Forage accumulated and saved in a pasture that is available for future grazing.

Substitute Feed — A feed that makes up for a deficiency in forage quantity. Feeding hay is substitute feeding. Substitute feeding generally decreases profit.

Supplemental Feed — A feed that makes up for a deficiency in forage quality. Ranchers commonly supplement forage with minerals and protein. Correct supplemental feeding generally improves gross margin per unit.

Terms Used in Section 2: Happy Families

Effectiveness Areas — A one-to-four-word statement describing the thing(s) for which a position is accountable (e.g., livestock production, forage production). Targets are assigned to effectiveness areas so that employee performance can be measured.

Mission Statement — A statement of why a business exists. A mission statement usually consists of two parts: a statement of purpose and a statement of core values.

Organization Chart — A diagram identifying the roles in a business and showing to whom those roles are assigned.

Paradigm — A set of assumptions, concepts, values, guidelines, and/or practices that constitutes the way someone sees and interprets things.

Vision Statement — A statement of what the business will look like and how it will operate at some point in the future. The vision statement describes how the business will accomplish its mission.

Terms Used in Section 3: Profitable Businesses

Benchmarks — A standard of success by which a business's performance can be measured and evaluated.

Breeding Herd Statistics Chart — A tool for estimating reproductive performance in a herd or flock.

Capital Expense — The money spent to purchase fixed assets or to add value to existing fixed assets.

Capitalizing — Divesting yourself of a fixed asset that is not producing income.

Concessionizing — Creating an ongoing stream of income from a fixed asset.

Cash Flow — A spreadsheet showing cash income and cash expenses. The cash flow shows how much and when (by month) money came in and out, what it came in for and what it was spent on.

Depreciation — The decrease in the value of an asset over time.

Direct Costs — Costs that increase or decrease directly as the units of production in an enterprise increase or decrease. In livestock enterprises, feed and health costs are direct costs.

Fixed Asset — Something with a useful life extending beyond the taxable year.

Gross Margin — The contribution an enterprise makes toward paying overhead costs and making a profit. Gross Product – Direct Costs = Gross Margin

Gross Margin Per Unit — The enterprise gross margin divided by the number of units in an enterprise. It measures the economic efficiency of an enterprise. The unit can be standard animal units, acres, dollars invested, rainfall, etc.

Gross Product — The economic value produced by an enterprise. Gross product is calculated using a "trading account." Gross product for livestock enterprises is: (Closing Herd Value + Livestock Sales) – (Livestock Purchases + Opening Inventory Herd Value) = Gross Product

Gross Product Per FTE — A key performance indicator for labor efficiency. It is calculated by dividing a business's total gross product by the total number of paid and unpaid full-time employee equivalents.

Key Performance Indicator — An indicator showing the economic or financial health of a business.

Livestock Valuation — A form used to record livestock inventory values. In economic planning, opening and closing values per head are held constant for each class of stock.

Non-Cash Costs — Things that reduce the value of your operation but don't show up in the cash flow (death loss, opportunity costs, unpaid labor, etc.).

Opportunity Cost — The value of the best alternative not taken. Opportunity rent on land is the rent that you could receive were you to rent your ranch to someone else. Your livestock operation should pay opportunity rent in this amount to your land business.

Overhead Costs — Costs that tend not to change as the units of production in an enterprise change (there are exceptions). All land, labor and administrative costs are overheads. Overhead costs are not included in the gross margin calculation.

Profit — Total Gross Margin - Overhead Costs = Profit

Profit or Loss Statement — A financial document showing a company's gross product, cash and non-cash costs and profit during a particular period. It can be used to project, or show actual, profit or loss. It is also known as an income statement.

Stock Flow Plan — A spreadsheet tracking changes in livestock inventory and projecting changes in herd structure. A stock flow shows the opening inventory, births, deaths, purchases, sales, transfers in and out of a class or enterprise, and the closing inventory.

Trading Account — The tool used to calculate gross product. A trading account adds livestock sales to the closing herd value and subtracts livestock purchases and the opening herd value.

Turnover — The total gross product produced by a business. It includes the number of units an enterprise produces and the number of enterprises.

Unpaid (or Underpaid) Labor — Labor that is not paid what it would cost to hire someone else to do the job. Unpaid labor must be accounted for in an economic analysis.

Working Capital — The money needed to operate the business. Items consumed the year they are purchased are included in working capital.

RMC

Ranch Management Consultants, Inc.

Healthy Land, Happy Families
and Profitable Businesses

To order more copies of Healthy Land, Happy Families and Profitable Businesses call (707) 429-2292 or visit www.ranchingforprofit.com.

Made in the USA
Columbia, SC
09 June 2019